Lessons Learned Through the Power of My Journey

Family Man, Entrepreneur, Civil Rights Activist

Jim Griffin

DEDICATION

This book is dedicated in loving memory to Cardrienne P. Griffin, my devoted late wife of sixty cherished years. The love of my Cardrienne as a loyal mother to our four children; Cheryl, Debbie, Jewel, and Malcolm and sons-in-law, Jay Threatt, Sr. and Dean Shannon, shines through eight grandchildren; Jay Jr., Jarvis, Jamal, Jasmine, Dominique, Jada, Sean and Coral, and two great-grandchildren; Riley and Jeremiah, who all affectionately called her 'Big Mama.' I could have searched the world and would never have discovered a more virtuous woman embodied by unassumed greatness. I also dedicate the writing of my story to my beloved and courageous daughter, Debbie Griffin Shannon. At the age of 51, Debbie left us too soon, yet her loving memory will never depart our hearts.

My Angels, Cardrienne and Debbie
Always in my heart! Gone but never forgotten!

I am also equitably grateful for the love and support of my parents, the late Rose and Richard, Griffin siblings: **The Late Richard Griffin**, Jr. (also known as Bangie) (the late Sue Griffin), Betty Walston, Roy, Brenda, Rickey, Denise, Jackie and Gregory Griffin; **Lawrence Griffin** (the late Iris Griffin), Michele Burley (godchild), (Ronald Burley), Michael Morton (Erica Morton), Shamikah and Noah Morton, Christopher Griffin Scott (Jameriez Scott); **The Late Katherine Blake** (the late Larry Blacke); **The Late Gladys Russell**, the late Reginald Russell (Brenda Russell), Michele and Michael Russell, Cabrina McLain (Melissa Saunders) Candace Myers; Sean Russell, Markis, Marquise, and Maya Russell; Tanya Russell, Michael Sean Russell, II, Karmen Russell, Tyler Khalid Kamille Murray; Tenaya Lewis, Anniya Lewis and Brandon Vandyver; The Late Sandra Corporal; Kim Lawal (Kamaru Lawal), Adeola, Kamaru and Adeyemi Lawall; Antoinese Toni) Watkins, Rachel Watkins; Jackie Kwegan (Andy Kwegan) Christopher (Lolade) Kwegan, Christina (Tililola) Kwegan; Crystal Corporal, Wendy Nance (Michael Nance), Saheed Shittu and Mishel Nance; Stacey Carter (Rico Carter); Laferne Johnson (Alan Johnson), Monocle Nole, Brittney Campbell (Brian Campbell) and Brian Campbell, Jr. and Kenny Walston; Marcus Quinn Nole (Trashawn Nole), Aurikshauna Ratliff, Ananda Nole and Marcus Quinn Nole, Jr.; Alton Russell (Elaine Rice); **The Late Elizabeth Fulwood** (Moses Fulwood); **The Late Ersell Griffin,** Jerryl Brown (Gisele Brown), Towanda Taylor, Gabrielle and Gabriel Taylor, Jerryl Brown Jr. Breonna Byrd, Jerryl, III, Morgyn, Khire, Keaira and Madison Brown, Kelley Brown, Kelbi Greene and Bryan Brown; Garry "Bo" Brown (Patricia Ann Brown), Jackie Brown (Amyah Turner), Shanelle Brown, Cai Perry, Janelle Brown, Janae Culmer and Keith Townes; Robbin Brown; Gregory Brown, Sr. (Patricia Brown), Gregory Brown, Jr. (Jenna Brown), Angel, Paige, Jazmine, Hailey and Mason Brown; Tisha Brown, Ciarra Miles, Caden Steward and Taylor Brown. **Viola Griffin.** My in-laws (the late Louise and Dr. Horace Perrin); my sister-in-law, the late Dr. Julia P. Davidson (Kevin, Taylor and Kyle Davidson), Larry Young, and Chanel Mosby. The Threatt's: Grace, Tony and Joanette (deceased) who became a special part of our family when Jay, Sr. and Cheryl married 33 years ago.

I'd be remiss if I didn't also thank all of my Fairmount Neighbors who are a beacon of light to me; fraternity brothers of Omega Psi Phi Fraternity, the Johnson C. Smith Alumni Chapter, Women Behind the Community; and other close friends who were in the struggle with me including: the late Walter P. and Zerita Carter (their children: Senator Jill P. Carter, Judy Carter-Sylvester and family), the late Mary Robinson and Charles Robinson, the late Roland and Marion Patterson (Roland and Doris Griffin), and many more close friends who have supported me over the years.

My heartfelt thanks to Cheryl and Jewel for continuing the legacy of Women Behind the Community, Inc. (WO-BE-CO). In memory of Cardrienne and Debbie.

Acknowledgements

Cheryl, *for inspiring me to write this book by saying, "Daddy you have done a lot, why not write a book."*

Jewel, *for doing most of the writing and prodding me to include my true feelings throughout the book.*

Malcolm, *for strengthening our Father-son bond to help me through tough times after Big Mama passed.*

Dominique and Coral *for support with typing and your kind words to encourage me.*

Jada, *for listening to my stories and the oral support during my weak moments.*

Jay Jr., Jarvis and Jamal, *for uplifting my spirits and always making me laugh.*

My entire Griffin family *especially, my brother (**Lawrence**), my niece/ goddaughter, **Michele** who checks on me often, niece, **LaFerne** for moral support and great niece **Crystal** who comes by to bring me food and listen to my stories. **Alton Russell**, for checking on me often and reminding me of some important memories for my book.*

Monica Thompson and Charles Ford, *for being more than good neighbors, they are an adopted family, whom I'm grateful for driving me everywhere I need to go and countless other acts of kindness.*

Jocelyn Labsi - *neighbor and adopted daughter who always helps with programs and anything else needed.*

Glynis and Vernon Ross, *my North Carolina extended family whose love and support continue to keep me strong throughout this time in my life*

Janet Branch, *my Virginia daughter who continues to support and encourage me.*

Rebertha Pope Matthews, *my other Virginia daughter who provided me guidance in writing this book and always available to give moral support and a prayer whenever needed.*

Lori Chambers and Sherri Adair, *my bonus Baltimore family who have provided tasty meals after Big Mama's passing.*

Sharronne Bryant, *who continues to encourage me since Big Mama's passing.*

Marcia Pope, *another adopted daughter who will help clean my house and do anything else needed.*

Wanda and Bill Brown *for support when needed.*

Chanel Mosby, *like another daughter, available to help when needed.*

Larry Young, *like another son, for your support over the years.*

Charles Robinson and Family, *an adopted brother who has supported me over many years.*

My brothers (and quettes) of Omega Psi Phi Fraternity, Inc., *Social Action Committee. Mel Fossett and Toni; Charles Simmons and Vanessa; Carlton and Francis Gordon;*

Dwayne White *for being a special fraternity brother.*

Special tennis buddies, *Dr. Harold Ramsey, William Garrett, Mickey Fields, Steve Ward.*

Tony and Grace Threatt, *Cheryl's* **in-laws** *who have been family for 33 yrs. and always present for family gatherings.*

Melody Harris, *Thank you for always uplifting us in your poetic style like only you can do.*

April Drummond, *Thank you for your creative design for the cover to the book.*

TABLE OF CONTENTS

FOREWORD

Jim Griffin aspired to succeed as a family man, civil rights activist, and entrepreneur. While Jim strived to overcome many setbacks and tribulations during his lifetime, one thing was sure: he never gave up. With hard work and determination, Jim persevered despite being victimized by numerous accounts of racism, a few failed business ventures, and being a black man at the height of atrocities in America. Through it all, he effortlessly remained kind, generous, and humble.

When turning this book's pages, one can learn the irreplaceable ingredients to succeed in love, life, and entrepreneurship. These lessons include the secret ingredient to marriage until "death do you part," how to balance the demands of having a successful business while maintaining family cohesiveness and unselfishly helping others, in turn, cultivating a positive impact on your community.

Jim Griffin's story, a toolbox for some of life's greatest lessons is for all generations. His memoirs are filled with personal accounts of good times, inspiration, and respect from family, longtime friends, and community associates. Charles Robinson, who has known Jim Griffin for over 50 years, regards him as a loyal friend who will do anything for anyone. Jim Griffin's life story is a testament to the power of dreams, hope, faith, love, and all lessons learned in between.

BIO

James Monroe Griffin ('Jim'), a native of East Baltimore, is a fighter for social justice and human rights. As chairman of the Congress of Racial Equality (CORE) 1963-1968, he led demonstrations against racial segregation in housing, employment, unions, and education. In 1968, Jim along with his wife, Cardrienne, had the vision to start Women Behind CORE which was later changed to Women Behind the Community (WO-BE-CO), Inc. WO-BE-CO's mission to empower women, children and families in the Baltimore Metropolitan area continues to flourish.

Jim Griffin was appointed to the Baltimore City Board of School Commissioners in 1968, serving through 1974. As Personnel Chairman, he demanded that African Americans be recognized and promoted to higher positions and treated fairly. He served briefly as the first African American Vice President and President of the Baltimore City School Board. He was appointed by the Mayor at that time to the Baltimore Model City Board and by former Governor Spiro Agnew as an Equal Opportunity Specialist.

He founded Griffin Associates, P.A., becoming the first African American in the state of Maryland with a private Physical Therapy (PT) practice. He mentored and trained countless PT students, encouraging them in their academic and professional pursuits. Jim is a member of Omega Psi Phi Fraternity, Incorporated, Pi Omega Chapter. He passionately served on the Social Action Committee. Under his tenure as chairman, in 1986, he helped establish the Principle Achievers Mentoring Program. The program provided mentoring and the experiences of African American males from ages 8 to 18. Under his leadership, he received the following awards: Superior Service Award, Bridge Builders, Founders Award, and Omega Man of the Year. From 1987-2001, Jim and his wife Cardrienne coordinated tours to Historically Black Colleges and Universities for students in the Baltimore Metropolitan Community. Jim served as a member of the Sojourner Douglass Board of Directors (for over twenty years); on the Advisory Boards of Walbrook High School; and, Epsilon Omega Foundation an affiliate of Alpha Kappa Alpha Sorority, Inc. He was inducted into the Dunbar High School and Johnson C. Smith University's Hall of Fame for his outstanding contributions to the community. After his first retirement, he started working for P.B. Health Home Care Agency where he worked part-time for 18 years up until June 2019. In his spare time, he loved playing tennis; as well as, watching tennis matches – especially the Williams sisters. Though his accomplishments are numerous, he is especially proud of being a devoted husband to his late wife, Cardrienne for 60 years, father "extraordinaire" to four children, loving role model and "Pop Pop" to eight grands and two great-grands.

PREFACE

My hero, the first man I ever loved, one who is a kind and gentle man that would do anything for you. That's my dad, Jim Griffin. Growing up as the oldest child, I observed first hand how he helped so many family members, students, friends and people on the street. He never met a stranger. If he saw someone on the street begging for money, he would stop and give it to them. When he worked as a rehabilitation counselor he would bring home ex cons, clients, anyone that needed a meal or his assistance. Always putting the needs of others before himself, it was nothing for dad to put money in his kids or grandchildren's account, assist someone who needed his financial help to further their education or just pay their bills. Our parents were always the ones who were at all of our functions and our house was where everyone gathered. They became adopted parents to our friends, providing listening ears and giving advise as needed. The greatest lesson my dad taught me was the willingness to help others in need especially those in the African American and underserved communities. As I followed in his footsteps, becoming a physical therapist, I am proud to be the child most like him. Today, I work in Home Health care and largely serve low - income communities. The compassion to go above and beyond to help educate and rehabilitate patients who often are unable to speak for themselves was instilled in me. Being a wife for 33 yrs and a dedicated parent of 2 black males in this day and time wasnt always easy. Thank you for being my role model and leading by example. Thank you for raising a daughter to be a strong black educated woman who is able to handle any problem and presevere. I am blessed to have had you for my dad.

Love, Your Oldest Daughter, Cheryl

My Dad is the rare essential ingredient of a selfless one hundred percent family man, combined with the voice of a freedom fighter, who helped eradicate social change in our community. He epitomizes a rare 'gem' teaching me by his example that "nothing gained without a struggle is worthwhile." As his youngest daughter, I observed him (along with my Mom by his side) put his heart and soul into making others' lives better while still providing for our family. What I admire most about him is that though he had his own business, served on countless boards and community organizations, he was home for family dinner by 6:00 pm every night. As a result of my Dad's influence, I learned to find my own voice in a world where women aren't supposed to have one. I've learned how to follow my dreams even when I was afraid to pursue them. I've learned how to spread my wings so that I can take flight and soar. I'm grateful for having a dad (and mom) who paved the way for me. He is the "wind beneath my wings."

Love, Jewel Griffin Linzey (AKA "Baby Girl")

My Dad is a very strong black man. An excellent family provider and supporter. He's always had my back through all the stupid things I've done growing up in a house full of women. The things he has accomplished are amazing to me. I'm working very hard to be somewhat just like him for which I know I will never be. However, I will sure as hell try cause there's nothing like being your own boss…and he is definitely his Own Boss.

Love Your Son, Mal

Above: Malcolm, Cheryl, Jewel and Jim

Below: Jewel, Malcolm, Debbie, Cheryl
at my 80th Birthday Party

INTRODUCTION

When I reflect on how far I've come, and from whence I came, it makes me want to pinch myself. I never dreamed or imagined that I would be given the opportunity to go to college, let alone on a football and track scholarship. To further my education on a higher level was surreal, especially since my parents could not afford to send me to college.

I'm fortunate to have been blessed with a wife who supported me every step of the way. Whether it was with my businesses or fighting against social injustices, she believed in what I was doing and worked with me or on her pursuits to uplift the black community.

We instilled in our children the importance of 'giving back' and helping others in need. We never sat them down to tell them what to do or even how to do it. Instead, we led by example. Uniquely different, each of our children have maintained a legacy of service. Collectively, they always made Cardrienne and I proud to be their parents.

I hope this book will inspire you to take a stand and fight for social justices that empower the lives of black people and uplift our communities. I am appalled as I write this book about the struggles that awakened my social consciousness, shaping who I am as a black man in white America. The same injustices I fought against for my children in the '60s are now right before my eyes. They have resurfaced to the forefront of my existence and sadly remain just as prominent for my grandchildren in 2021.

CHAPTER ONE

NEVER FORGET WHERE YOU CAME FROM

"In America, it is difficult to be your own man."
Sidney Poitier

MY HUMBLE BEGINNINGS:

I came into manhood through the lens of my people.

As I think back to one warm summer day in East Baltimore in 1955, home from college, I will never forget having to bail my father out of jail. He spent three weeks in prison for running illegal numbers. The $2,000 bail money was given to me by the person who backed his hustle. This was a time when Blacks were not able to get loans to operate businesses from banks. If you ever heard of Willie Adams (Little Willie Adams) from Baltimore, a former numbers runner who became a successful venture capitalist, the culture of this era would be undeniable.

I grew up during the height of America's Great Depression: a time of uncertainty in a place where it was hard to be black, let alone a black man. Born at 8:10 a.m. on the eleventh day of March 1932 to Richard Griffin (Crew, VA) and Rosa Royal (Blackstone, VA) resided at 1815 E. Eager Street in Baltimore, Maryland. Given the name James Monroe Griffin at birth, I prefer to be called 'Jim.' It is interesting, yet unclear, why my parents named me after James Monroe, the fifth president of the United States of America.

There were nine of us living in a three-story, four-bedroom home. We later found out that my father had another family down the street, and at age 67, my dad had his 8th child, Viola. It was not until my late adult years that we fully accepted her as our sister.

I never imagined until now what pressure, not to mention fears, my parents must have felt raising children at that time. Yet somehow, we survived despite a diminishing economy, joblessness, and homelessness echoing all around us. I conjure this made it even more perplexing for many black boys, like me, growing up to find our place in a world that didn't embrace or respect us.

We struggled against taking the path of least resistance into manhood. There were few opportunities for us to grab hold of, which left blacks (especially those who had little to no education) with their backs up against a wall, fighting for the survival of our families and ourselves. Grappling with our perseverance, this was a confusing time, marked with 'the last hired, first fired,' and two to three times more likely than whites to be unemployed. The reality for my siblings and me, the plight of our existence all around the streets of inner-city Baltimore and plagued across America, brought despair. As categorized, the Great Depression manifested a profound negative impact on black families that was endured for ten years. My family was no exception.

My mother worked as a housekeeper for the Mayor of Baltimore and my dad, who only had a 3rd-grade education, ran (illegal) street numbers for horse racing to support us. Many families in our communities made their living this way. If business was good, he would give us lunch money for school. If not, we were out of luck and had to get lunch the best way possible. On those days, I would ask anyone at school for spare change so I could eat.

Baltimore had two prominent gangs at that time, Broomstones and Vikings. We would often watch them from our home as they were gang banging. My sister Katherine's first marriage was to a gangster who was in and out of jail so much she finally divorced him. Living in what is often referred to as the "Ghetto" or the "Hood" and around constant violence became part of my motivation to pursue college. These experiences and more provided lessons that would positively motivate my existence to produce better. I also wanted to prove to my community that I did not have to follow in my father's footsteps and unlawfully support a family. I would break this cycle by becoming a college graduate to help my family and give back to the community. I accepted that I lived in poverty, and I escaped its perils, but not without a few distinct childhood adventures.

One of my most vivid memories as a child (which changed the course of my life) was when my parents bought me a pair of skates at age ten. Even though my Mom told me not to go out of the neighborhood on my skates, it fell on deaf ears. I was your typical rambunctious 'knucklehead' who didn't listen. I did just the opposite and went skating around the corner about three blocks. Filled with the adrenaline rush of skating downhill came to a screeching halt when my frail body was hit by a moving car and instantly knocked me into a chicken coup. Before I knew it, I was rushed to Johns Hopkins Hospital. I had to get a cast put on my left forearm and wrist. I spent several weeks going to Johns Hopkins to receive treatment for my fractured left wrist. This childhood trauma later ensued into my life's passion for an innate desire to help others in need. When I had to decide on a major to pursue in college, I vividly remembered the specialized care and treatment I received as a child at Johns Hopkins. It provoked my interest in wanting to become a recreational therapist, which in time evolved as a physical therapist.

Growing into Manhood (High School years):

"James was always soft-spoken and aware of others' feelings and willing to help whenever possible. I'm proud to have him as a friend and most proud to call him brother".

Lawrence Griffin

My brother, Lawrence, recounts growing up in the 1930s in a family of nine wasn't easy, but we managed to get it done with relative ease. As my younger brother, he recalls us having different sets of friends, so we hardly ever saw one another until after dark when it was time to come in for the night. We have been competitors since childhood, but we played on the same team once we entered high school.

We played football and ran track for Dunbar High School in Baltimore, Maryland. We had the honor to participate in the Penn Relays as a quartet with teammates James Ralph and William White. We didn't win but considered it a privilege to be invited.

Lawrence was offered a track scholarship to attend Wisconsin University but turned it down to accept a scholarship at Morgan State College. During his second year, he injured his leg while on the track team. Morgan's coaches would not hold his scholarship while he was injured, and he could no longer afford to stay in school. After leaving school, he got married and they had a baby girl (Michele). Before getting injured, Lawrence was one of the fastest men on the team; in fact, he was Olympic material.

Even though we were star athletes, we were not indifferent to the behavior of a typical teenager. One day, after playing basketball and drinking beer, Sidney, myself, and another friend, decided to go walking and singing around the neighborhood.

While we walked and sang, the three of us suddenly challenged each other to smash a couple of windows by hitting them with our fists. I went first and pulled my fist back and struck a lady's window with full force and quickly pulled it back without hurting my hand. Our friend did the same thing. When he pulled his fist back, his wrist got caught in a piece of glass, and blood flew everywhere. He had cut a blood vessel in that wrist. We rushed him to the nearby hospital for immediate treatment. Our friend's hand and wrist were forever weakened. I learned never to do something like that on a foolish whim.

There were times when my family and I were exposed to the upper echelon of society which influenced me greatly. My mother was the housekeeper and sister Elizabeth cooked for the Mayor of Baltimore Thomas Delasandro Jr.'s family of politicians. My sister was a good soul food cook, well known for her fried chicken. I ran errands for their family during my junior and senior years at Dunbar. I was not paid monetarily; however, my volunteer commitment influenced the Delasandros to recommend me for a summer job in the city's Department of Transportation as a clerk. In order to secure the job, I had to become a Democrat which gave me my first exposure to politics. Our families, although from two different spectrums of society, were intertwined. I became acquaintances with Thomas Delasandro III ('Young Tommy') we were a year apart in age. He is the brother of the current Speaker of the House Nancy Pelosi (Delasandro). Being indirectly a part of their lavish lifestyle inspired me to want to achieve more out of life.

CHAPTER TWO

NOTHING GAINED WITHOUT A STRUGGLE IS WORTHWHILE

When I think of my Grandfather, I think of a...
Black Man..
Strong wise black man
The strength to hold a fountain together
The type to soak up the rain
for his family beyond umbrella;
The black man that guides the family;
The black man who's wise words build up
every other black man coming behind him;
The black man who teaches the woman in his life
what a real black man is supposed to be.
Black man, we love you
for the things you've done.
We love you for the battles
we thought we lost but actually won;
The true definition of a black
strong and wise black man.
Jasmine Griffin (Granddaughter)

Setbacks and Triumphs (College Years):

My life began to change for the better when my High School Football Coach William, 'Sugar' Cain, asked my best friend Sidney Raines and me to visit him. We thought we were in trouble, but to our surprise, he informed us about a football scholarship offered by Johnson C. Smith University's (JCSU) football coach Jack Brayboy.

A Central Intercollegiate Athletic Association (CIAA) colleague of his, Coach Jack Brayboy, of JCSU, needed several football players. To our surprise, he recommended Sidney and me. Both of us received athletic scholarships, Sidney, as linebacker and myself as wide receiver. We were an indomitable force to be reckoned with.

The mere thought of leaving Baltimore to attend college was indeed a game-changer for us. Without a doubt, we accepted the offer, and in the late summer of August 1950, off to JCSU we went: two black boys leaning on the shoulders of Dunbar High School giants who saw more in us than we did in ourselves. We were so excited and humbled by the fact that JCSU Athletic Director, Coach Byrd Crudup, who was from Baltimore, gave us a ride to JCSU. I was proud to be attending an Historically Black College and University (HBCU). From Baltimore to North Carolina, we traversed into unknown, unchartered territories. Afraid yet filled with the excitement of what was to come.

With all my belongings in just one suitcase, I did not let the emptiness of a devoid childhood deter me. I may have been poor in worldly possessions, but I was rich in promise. Never did I envision that I'd trade city life for the confines of country southern living. Not even in my wildest dreams did I ever think that I'd be afforded a chance to go to college -- let alone on a football scholarship. It turned out I earned more than I imagined. I was chosen 'best athlete' in my class and received a $5.00 gift certificate. Unfortunately, there was no additional money for this highly costly award, but to this day I remain grateful.

Sidney and I had very little money, but we met some good down to earth people who really looked out for us. Folks, like Howard Petty, who worked in the printing shop at JCSU. He provided printed food stamps, which allowed us to eat regularly. We were able to survive by Howard Petty, friends, and teammates providing us with food and so much more. I managed to pay JCSU a token amount towards my tuition and Sidney's. I paid $10.00 on my bill and $5.00 for Sidney. It felt good to have enough money to sustain myself and some leftovers to help another brother out. Although my parents couldn't afford to send me money, my brother Bangie sent me $36.00 a month for 3 years, and my sister Katherine would help by purchasing clothes and items for school.

I had the pleasure of being roommates with Harvey Key for freshman, sophomore and junior year. We were like brothers and looked out for each other. Harvey reminded me that the best way to describe us was "poor struggling college students". Nearly all of us who stayed in Carter Hall had to exchange clothes and suit jackets to help one another out from time to time. He used to tease me about how much I ate. He said, I'd eat everything on my plate and everyone else's, too. Though I was slender in statue, I could devour a lot of food and not gain any weight. I took special care to make sure that I stayed fit then (and now) always being conscientious about caring for my body. Both of us were on the track team together so it was imperative that we stayed in shape. Harvey was nicknamed 'the rabbit' after his style of running. He described me as the epitome of a star athlete since I played by the coaches' rules and worked hard to sharpen my skills. According to him, if Coach Byrd Crudup said: "run it out", I would run it out even if I had a headache, body ache, or any kind of ailment - I'd do what he said. Lots of mischievous times were had by Harvey and me with unmentionable secrets between us.

Whenever it was time to leave the campus for the Christmas holiday, I'd get a dull feeling. It meant giving up my newly found independence in the unobtrusive country lifestyle back to the qualms of city life. When I was home during the summer between my second and third year from JCS, a friend of mine asked me to walk downtown with him to consider buying some clothes. We stopped in a clothing store and were looking at socks. Suddenly, he picked up a handful of socks and shoved them between my left shoulder and left chest areas. I clamped down on them to prevent them from falling on the floor. I kept the socks, and we left the store, unaware the store manager saw the incident. We walked a short distance from the store, and suddenly I felt someone pulling on my belt and said I was under arrest for stealing the socks. Meanwhile, my friend was running his mouth, challenging the police. The store manager came on the scene and learned that I didn't steal the socks. I convinced him that I was a college student on vacation and had no intention of stealing anything. He persuaded the policeman to let me go. That day, I learned a valuable lesson: to be careful who your friends are and be observant of the actions of those in your presence. This could have changed the trajectory of my life for the worst. Thank God it didn't!

The 1950s brought with it a time of agony and indecisiveness for black people. Yet, at that time, the struggles of my people were oblivious to me as a college student. I'll never forget when it was time to return to school - Sidney's family couldn't convince him to go back. On the other hand, my parents insisted that I did. They were focused on the need for me to leave the plight that was so prominent for blacks in Baltimore. They desired to see my siblings and me without the anguish and limitations that plagued our people.

I went back to JCSU but was three days late. Upon return to class, I was summoned out of class and suspended for two weeks. I learned another valuable lesson that day: to obey the rules. College rules and regulations were stringent at that time. It became critical for me to get the city slicker mentality out of my spirit and march to a different drum. Luckily, I had the support of my family and good grades, which allowed me to retain my scholarship. I continued my matriculation at Johnson C. Smith University until the end of my third year, remaining on campus as a hall monitor.

Troubles surfaced while I was having fun, drinking liquor and beer with schoolmates. One day, to my surprise, Dean Grimes appeared at my front door. My schoolmates alerted me about Dean's presence, but too late. I muttered, "Fuck the Dean," left, and went to bed. The next day, Dean Grimes expelled me from Johnson C. Smith University. To be indefinitely separated from JCSU felt like a death sentence. All my hopes and dreams of becoming the first in my family to graduate from college suddenly seemed insurmountable.

After leaving school in the late summer of 1953, I was drafted into the Army and summoned to Camp Gordon, Georgia. During my trip to Georgia, I was the only African American on the bus. When the driver stopped for lunch in Lynchburg, Virginia, everyone except me could sit and eat in the restaurant. This was my first experience with racism that denied me of what should have been an equal right. However, during that time, I was merely disappointed and didn't understand the disparity engulfing me.

Another incident of racism occurred in the Army while playing touch football with mostly white players. I would run up and down the field looking to receive a ball that was intentionally never thrown my way. Although I had the speed and skill of playing college football as a wide receiver, the quarterback overlooked my position every time.

 In reflection of the previously mentioned experiences, it wasn't until I was discharged from the Army I realized I had been discriminated against, time and time again. I was incredibly naive to the social and cultural injustices of what was happening to and all around me.

I served twenty-two months as a soldier at Camp Gordon. I was trained in the Army to be a cable splicer and hated every moment. However, I persevered through to complete special leadership courses and other activities while in the service. After basic training, I attended another 13-week leadership course. This course set a strong foundation for the trials and tribulations which I have endured in life. I'm sure it also helped me become an effective leader in all of my endeavors.

Upon completing the leadership course, I remained on base because I was afraid to go into town due to the racism and hard times waiting for African American soldiers from Camp Gordon. I didn't visit the closest locality, Augustus, Georgia, from September to April because of the fear of what could happen to me as a black soldier. I knew it would not be a good idea to subject myself to the atrocities in Augustus.

While in the Army, I did not give up on trying to get back into college. I would visit Johnson C. Smith and talk with Dean Grimes on numerous occasions. I admired the principles he stood for but remained saddened due to his unwavering position of not allowing me to return as a student of JCSU. I used everything I could to appeal to him. I even tried to stimulate his empathy and pride as an Omega man because I had previously gone through the Lampados Pledge Club. Unfortunately, that thought process proved me wrong. Dean Grimes, once again, remained steadfast in his decision. Nonetheless, it didn't matter since my time in the Lampados Pledge Club was cut short. I didn't have the $185 needed to continue the process, which at that time was a lot of money. My big sister, Katherine, who often helped me with my college expenses, couldn't loan me the money. She was scheduled for an operation and was concerned about the costs she would incur. I was disappointed, but at the same time I understood my sister's health was more important to me. With persistence and fortitude, I continued to make frequent visits to Dean Grim's office on the weekends. I can't count the number of times I sat out in front of his office begging him to let me back into school. I reiterated that I would live up to every one of the four cardinal principles (manhood, scholarship, perseverance, and uplift). I also informed him if I needed additional principles to rejoin the JCSU family, not to hesitate to add them. I even wrote him several long letters and told him I wouldn't cuss anymore.

Finally, the day of reckoning arrived. He was either very tired of me as a fixture in his office or I convinced him to allow me back in school, because I was changed. It seemed forever before I was finally released from the Army. I requested and was granted an early honorable discharge.

With much gratitude, I returned to Johnson C. Smith University in August of 1955, three semesters away from a college degree. Upon returning, I was faced with another one of life's lessons. An incomplete grade in Physics, which was a required course for my double major in General Science and Physical Education had been changed to a C. I don't know why I got a C - I thought it was a God of mercy. This was my wake-up call. At that point, I buckled down, studied hard, and became an honor student for the first time. With tenacity and purpose, I continued pursuing a double major in General Science and Physical Education.

CHAPTER THREE

CHERISH LOVE AND FAMILY

I spent many weekends with my Pop Pop and we enjoyed watching Tyler Perry Madea movies and had so many good times. I just love my Pop Pop. **Sean Griffin (Grandson)**

As the youngest grandchild to Pop Pop, I look up to him for many different reasons. Pop Pop (and Big Mama) showed me the value of being supportive towards your family. They would always support me at my dance shows, pageants, and school activities. I admire Pop Pop's work ethic and his discipline in being health conscious. He taught me the importance of working hard. **I Love You, Coral Linzey (Granddaughter)**

HOW I MET MY TRUE LOVE:

Before graduating from Johnson C. Smith in Charlotte, North Carolina, my good friend Leon Watkins asked me to go along with him to visit his girlfriend Amanda Renwick and meet her friend, Mary Ann. It turned out Mary Ann had no interest in me at all. Instead, upon seeing Amanda's second roommate, Cardrienne, I was struck by her demeanor and innocence.

I never imagined she would be the love of my life. When I first saw her, I thought she was a little stockier than I usually went for, but after getting to know Cardrienne, it was something special about her, so nothing else mattered. Every time I was around her, she made me feel invincible.

Cardrienne was a teacher in an elementary school in Charlotte, North Carolina. Born in Atlanta, Georgia, and raised in Raleigh, North Carolina, she was a country girl at heart. She had the southern grace of an affluent Christian family yet was extremely down to earth. It was both her sophistication and wit that attracted me to her.

Unbeknownst to me, she came from a lineage of professional clergymen and educators. Through our courtship, I discovered that she was the granddaughter to a well-known prelate. In fact, her Grandfather, the late Rev. Dr. William A Fountain, served as a Bishop in the African Methodist Episcopal (AME) Church for 50 years and later served as President of Atlanta, Georgia's Morris Brown College, for which an historic academic building, Fountain Hall, was named in his honor.

Her father, Dr. Horace C. Perrin, was a Chemistry Professor at Morgan State College and her Mother, Louise Fountain Perrin, was a counselor at Coppin State College. She had one older sister, Dr. Julia Davidson, who held many professional positions. Julia served as Shaw University's Director of Alumni Relations and as Founder/Director of the NYUBURU (which means 'freedom house' in Swahili) Center that provided academic counseling and tutoring for minority students at the University of Maryland at College Park.

Cardrienne and I would talk for hours about our upbringing. Our worlds were different, but our souls connected. I remember visiting the Fountain home on Boulevard Street in Atlanta. I was in awe at how big their house was. They lived in the same Atlanta Auburn neighborhood as Dr. King's family. Cardrienne, in her younger years, was courted by Dr. Martin Luther King, Jr.'s youngest brother, Alfred Daniel (A.D.) King.

Cardrienne shared many stories with me about her entitled life as the Bishop's granddaughter. I'd laugh nonstop as she would tell how, as children, she and Julia would 'cut-up' as they sat on display often having to sit on the front row at church for the public. They were representing the first family, adorned in their fancy dresses with big bows hanging from long home-styled curly-locked hair. One of the funniest stories was when they were required to participate in the church holiday play. To her embarrassment, the two sisters, devoid of vocal ability, had to each perform a solo in front of the entire congregation. Yet, to their surprise, they would get tons of compliments from members knowing they couldn't carry a note. After being blessed with such rich childhood experiences, her parents eventually migrated from the south - Raleigh, North Carolina, to Baltimore, Maryland, to begin a new chapter.

Although our upbringing was different, Cardrienne was subjected to the ills of segregation just like the rest of us black folk. We'd share stories of what it meant to be black in America and our awful experiences. I recall Cardrienne disclosing she was only allowed to go to the theatre on Sundays and since she was black was forced to go upstairs in the balcony to watch movies.

After we dated for a few years, Cardrienne and I wed on the twenty-first day of June 1958, at Bethel A.M.E. Church. Although the day was rainy, it was in every way you could imagine, a day filled with sunshine. I never envisioned our two different worlds would come together, and we would fall in love. It felt like a dream come true.

Family, friends, and special guests adorned us with their presence and gifts. One of our most cherished gifts is a plaque that still hangs in our home from former Baltimore Mayor and Mrs. Thomas Delasandros, Jr. presented to us for our wedding that reads: *"Mr.*

and Mrs. James M. Griffin, June 21, 1958 heartiest congratulations and best wishes on your wedding day. May almighty God shower you with his choicest blessings, and may you always have health, happiness and prosperity." This solidified the Griffin's and Delasandros' family ties at that time.

Making Sacrifices For My Future:

When it was time for me to graduate' from Johnson C. Smith, the thought that I wanted to pursue another degree was difficult for some to understand. While my brother Bangie who supported me in college and came to my graduation, he couldn't believe I was considering furthering my education. As we were standing in front of the Administration building, he looked at Cardrienne and said, "I should slap you cause Jim's going back to college and I know you are responsible for this."

When the time came for me to leave North Carolina to attend Boston University for a year, my Cardrienne decided to move to Baltimore with her parents. This became a joint sacrifice and the best way for me to pursue a certificate degree in Physical Therapy in Boston, Massachusetts, while knowing Cardrienne would be well cared for. The first day I arrived on campus, I met three white male fellows and one African American fellow. I received my class schedule consisting of 21 credits. I immediately realized I would have to study more than ever to pass and keep up with the white guys. I was taught early as a black boy never to let a white boy beat me at anything. To my surprise, after a few days in my classes, the competition became friendly between all of us. We formed a unified diverse team and started competing against the female students for better grades.

The classes were difficult, with homework assigned almost every night. I lived in Miles Standish Hall across from the Boston Gardens, the famous basketball arena. Regretfully, I couldn't afford to attend the Boston Celtics games, nor did I have time because of my demanding schedule.

The year studying at Boston University was challenging. My workload was 21 credits instead of the average 16-18 credits. I attended classes on a daily basis from 9:00 a.m. to 5:00 p.m. and back to my dormitory room for further study around 9:00 p.m. Despite the curriculum's extensive rigor, I made reasonably good grades, until it came to the source of my contingency, Electrotherapy. Electrotherapy was necessary, and I was failing miserably.

The Instructor, I believed, was a woman of European descent. It was because of the interest she showed in me that I was able to get through this class with a passing grade. When returning to the campus of Boston University after twenty years, I discovered my saving grace was actually an African American who had been the only woman of color, in the Physical Therapy Department.

When thinking of my time spent in Boston attending the University, I can't help but recall one unique experience when Cardrienne came up for the weekend to visit. Her outfit, a brown and white pleated dress, made her look country, as many would say when one has no sense of style. Without thinking, I made fun of the dress and told her I would ask my sister Katherine to show her how to dress appropriately when we returned to Baltimore. Cardrienne was upset and turned off by me. Therefore, I learned early in our union that if I were to have her as my Queen for a lifetime, to never criticize her about her clothing or anything else.

THE JOYS OF FAMILY:

Aside from love and marriage, one of life's richest rewards is being a father. Our four children had unique personalities indicative of how they arrived in the world. First, there was the oldest, Cheryl, born during a cold, blustery snowstorm on the thirteenth day of February 1960. At the time, we were living at 3412 Bateman Avenue. Cardrienne found the energy to get on her knees and scrub the kitchen floor late that evening. Shortly afterward, we drove in a snowstorm toward Johns Hopkins in our 1953 Chrysler in anticipation of welcoming our first child. I started out to an Amoco gas station on Tiago and Gwynns Falls Parkway, only to run out of gas prior to reaching the station. I called my Mother and Father-in-law to help because they lived nearby at 2004 Whittier Avenue. I started out again, headed to Johns Hopkins. To my dismay, it stopped running on Madison Street near Johns Hopkins. I was lucky to hail a cab and get to Johns Hopkins. An attendant met us at the Wolfe Street entrance, where Cardrienne was helped into a wheelchair and taken to the delivery room. I sat in the waiting room only a few minutes before a nurse informed me my first girl was born. Since that night, we later nicknamed Cheryl 'motor butt', which fits her until this very day. Cheryl never likes to sit still and is always ready for an adventure. True to life as the oldest child, she directs all of us on how to do things from what to wear and how to organize our homes.

Our second born, Debbie, arrived with a bang two years later on a warm summer day, the thirtieth day of May 1962. I was attending a meeting (somewhere I can't recall), and a call came for me to go to Sinai Hospital quickly – it was time for my second daughter's delivery. I barely arrived at the hospital in time for the arrival of our second daughter to be born. Again, not long afterward, Debra was born, yearning for our attention. She was your typical middle child – the glue that held our family together with her wit and charm.

Four years later, without much fanfare, our youngest daughter, Jewel, was born in the fall on the nineteenth day of October 1966. What made this experience different was that Cardrienne decided to stay at home from work indefinitely. She kept stretching it out. I didn't rush her to go back to teaching because my income was adequate to take care of our family. Jewel was referred to as our 'baby girl' not just for obvious reasons, but because she was privy to the extra love and attention, she received from Cardrienne due to her extended six-year maternity leave. It's probably why she takes after Cardrienne a lot when it comes to the way she approaches work with precision with an innate style of leadership that mimics her mother.

On the twenty-seventh day of September 1969, after having three girls the same height and weight, 6 pounds 4 ounces, it was time for a boy. It was a delight to have another male in the family. I wanted to name him Malcolm X, but Cardrienne would not allow it: so, we settled on just Malcolm. As the only boy, he makes sure his opinion is always heard. Malcolm takes pride in being the 'Mr. Fix-it' of our family. He is very protective of us all – especially his sisters. If any of them call him to fix something he is there in a heartbeat to help them out. I marvel how he can practically fix anything around the house or car. Now, of course, he went to auto mechanic school, but even before that - fixing things came natural to Malcolm. We have all come to depend on him to put things back together while at the same time, have come to expect him to give us a lecture afterwards on how to do everything the *right* way.

I met fatherhood head-on, not looking for a 'how-to' rule book but with humility and pride. Because I didn't have a lot growing up, I wanted to embellish our four children with more than I had but still not overdo it. I was frugal. I would give the children a limit on the cost of tennis shoes not to exceed $25, for example. Over the years, the children would tease me and say that I started recycling long before it became popular. I recall when Cardrienne's Aunt Sue came to visit us from Atlanta. She was an accomplished musician. At dinner, she asked for a napkin. I split a paper towel in half and gave her one side. Cardrienne and the children gasped in disbelief. While they were accustomed to my thriftiness, they couldn't believe that I'd give Aunt Sue, of all people, half a paper towel. As a quintessential woman of southern style and grace, she politely gestured a palatable nod of disapproval.

Years later, I recall when Cheryl was 16, to my surprise, she ate about 4 or 5 pork chops in one sitting. Afraid of the grocery bill being too high, from that day forward, I became a pescatarian. Soon afterward, I did my research on the health implications of not eating red meat and adopted the Activist and Comedian Dick Gregory's Bahamian Diet way of juicing fruits and vegetables. I tried to get Cardrienne to give up meat, but she loved her kosher hot dogs, pig feet, and southern barbeque too much. She supported me, though, by always cooking separate meals for me. I tried to persuade the children over the years, but to no avail. I even resorted to bribing them by offering money if they'd give up meat. Debbie and Jewel jumped at the challenge, but they didn't last long.

Cardrienne was accustomed to her side of the family living lavishly, and they loved to shop. Her Mother was stylish and wouldn't leave the house without her shoes, purse, and jewelry matching. Everyone called her 'Mama Lou'. She was a sweet church lady but, was not to be messed with. If the children got out of line, she would politely say 'I'm going to get my ruler' (that was more like the size of a yard stick) and they would shape up. Mama Lou was smart and talented, too. She was an Opera singer who had made several albums. Cardrienne would purchase finer things, but I was very fortunate she was good with her money. She would balance her checkbook down to the penny and pay credit card purchases before interest accrued. We would carefully weigh out the pros and cons of each major purchase against our tight budget.

Early on, Cardrienne and I decided to maintain separate bank accounts. I took care of all the costly household bills. She paid for groceries, gifts, and things for the children. Cardrienne had free reign to do what she wanted to do with the household income. That way, there was no debate or discrepancies. This worked for us. She would consult with me to make sure I agreed on any necessary home items. Well, except one time in our marriage, she went off on her own without consulting with me first. I came home from work one day to find a centralized electrical air conditioning unit with roughly a $3,400 price tag. I was a bit perturbed that day not only because she did not wait for my approval and it was also way over our budget. Nevertheless, Cardrienne had a way of convincing me of why we needed it. I was conscientious about taking care of my family's financial needs and paying bills swiftly. I paid a 30-year $12,500 mortgage ($125/month) in less than ten years. When I got involved in CORE, I wanted to make sure Cardrienne and my children would be well taken care of in the event something happened to me. I'd put the extra lump sum of money I made doing home health care towards the mortgage to cut it way down.

Fatherhood was met with various challenges. It was often a juggling act, whether running my own business full-time or being involved in the community, but I made a vow to Cardrienne to put family first no matter what was going on. I tried to honor this commitment by ensuring I was home for family dinner every night by 6:00 p.m. This was the designated time Cardrienne established for dinner and for us to come together to attend all our children's special events.

For the most part, my children were pretty good growing up, but we had the usual teenage problems, arguments, and disagreements. We survived those years with discipline, love, and support.

My children got along very well although each child had their own distinct personality. People say the oldest, Cheryl, looks just like me and is the most like me. She was always the mouthy child who always had to have the last word. She was the one who was in trouble the most and got spanked and her mouth slapped. One night, she was sitting in her room in her robe, and I told her to take a bath. I went downstairs and stayed awhile and when I returned, she was sitting in the same spot with her robe on. Of course, I spanked her. She yelled, "Dad, I did take my shower!" I stopped spanking her but then said, "well, that was a beating I should have given you for something else," and walked away.

Debbie, two years younger than Cheryl, would try to keep up, and hang out, with her big sis. She would tell you how she really felt without skipping a beat. Debbie enjoyed hanging out late with her friends and didn't hesitate to tell us about it. I remember one time she was in the attic in her room and had been smoking cigarettes and was dropping the butts out the window. When she got caught, she told her Mom, "you smoke so why can't I?" Cardrienne was speechless.

Jewel, who we called 'baby girl' never got a spanking. She was quiet, rather shy, and usually sat up under her Mom. She loved to read, write, and draw. She really liked school. She would play school in her room by herself with imaginary kids. It was rare she spoke up but if it was something she believed in, Jewel would find a way to get her way. I would try to pass down Cheryl and Debbie's clothes to her, but she wouldn't have it. She convinced me it wasn't fair that just because she was the youngest didn't mean she didn't deserve to get new clothes. There was the time, at the Debbie Shop on Reisterstown Road, when Jewel talked me into getting her two coats instead of one because she liked both of them. She would look up at me with those big bashful eyes and I'd give in to her wish.

Malcolm, AKA 'baby boy', oftentimes was moody trying to find a space surrounded with all the women. He was happy to finally get brothers-in-law.

As a child, Malcolm played little league baseball, and in his adult years' played and coached softball faithfully for James Mosher. He was a smart child, but didn't seem to get challenged enough in school. He gave college a try – one year at Virginia State University, but college wasn't for him. He got bored. Instead, he got certifications in auto mechanic, industrial mechanic, general contractor, and was a truck driver. I remember when he was 14 and came in late, I was fussing with him at the top of the steps, and he mouthed off. I grabbed him and he resisted me trying to spank him. He was stocky and strong. He said, "no disrespect, Dad but

I'm not going to let you hit me." It was that day that I realized I couldn't give him any more spankings.

We spent a lot of time with Cardrienne's sister Julia and her son Kevin, who I took under my wings like another son. He often speaks of me looking out for him and giving him manly advice including, on fatherhood to his children: Taylor and Kyle.

According to him, "growing up in a single-parent household in the '60s was not the best."

As the years passed, Kevin shared with me that he attributes the help of family as the recipe for survival. I didn't teach him about sports, but I just showed up in his life as a positive male role model making sure he had everything he needed. He also observed that I supported all my nieces and nephews on both sides of our family – the Perrins and Griffins. We invited Julia and Kevin to the Griffin's family gatherings, as we considered them a part of our extended family.

Kevin expressed his gratitude for me providing him with his first car in 1976 when he attended college at North Carolina Central University (NCCU). He was living off-campus his junior year and needed transportation. Since I had a reliable family car, I offered him my 1968 Volkswagen Beetle station wagon. Little did I know I'd receive a call from him telling me it broke down 20 miles into the trip back to school. Kevin was able to get the car fixed enroute and finally made it to North Carolina. We laughed about this later, and he was still more than thrilled to have had a car that helped him get started with his independence. He thought it was cool since no one else on NCCU's campus had a car like his. They stopped making this edition. Kevin thought he was a big shot, and it didn't help that I had it painted orange!

Throughout college, Kevin would call me for advice to make sure he was doing what was needed to be successful. Even after college, he would turn to me on occasion for wisdom. We had long conversations about nearly everything. Whether it was the little things, like the time I suggested he get a lawnmower so he wouldn't have to keep using his neighbor's, or big challenges like when Cardrienne and I extended our assistance to him. Our support was appreciated when his marriage folded. We did our best to instill in him so he would survive the transition positively.

I made sure to be there for both sides of our family. My niece, Laferne, recalls when she graduated from high school, she planned to go to college. To her surprise, one day I showed up with a check made out to Baltimore City Community College from Cardrienne and me to cover her first semester tuition. She wasn't sure what her financial plan was, but that solved it. She was going to college in September.

Laferne thinks I also had a lot to do with her getting hired at Model Cities that summer, where she met Walter Carter. That was a good experience for her to listen and learn of his philosophy.

Laferne graduated from Baltimore City Community College and later completed a bachelor degree at the University of Baltimore, became a Certified Public Accountant, and then obtained a master degree at Loyola College. I was really proud of her accomplishments. According to Laferne, I never missed an opportunity to stress the importance of education, always encouraged the younger generation in our family to tap into their individual gifts and was there to support them when they did. She further marveled that in addition to family, I helped any person striving to do better through entrepreneurship. Helping family has meant everything to me. I believe that my nephews, Garry and Jerryl were influenced by me to develop their own company.

My nephew, Alton Russell said, "y'all were the Cosby's and we were Good Times." Every opportunity we had to get together we tried to ensure both sides of our families were invited. Alton stated there was a class difference in my immediate family and the Griffin family. He recalls when Aunt Cardrienne was first being introduced to the family that his mom Gladys bought them new clothes and made them practice how they were going to speak, because they knew of her upbringing. Many times Alton and his sister, Laferne spent the night at our house. When he walked into our house, which seemed big to him, he saw nothing but African American Art inside. Alton stated he was amazed because he didn't see that in any other home. That was his first introduction to black culture.

Alton recounts how his Aunt Cardrienne would insist that everyone eat dinner together, have dinner conversation and could not get up until everyone had eaten their food. No music or TV was allowed during dinner. Then after dinner, you would do homework and read. This was not what he was accustomed to at his house. There was no structure like this in his home. Alton enjoyed coming over to our house. He recounts that one of his fondest memories of all time, was when he was forced to go to a Father-Son affair with me. He didn't want to wear a tux, but was made to wear it at 10 years old. Always being a rebel, he resisted but had to wear it and go anyway. Alton states, "it turned out to be one of the best times of my life". Over the years watching my political career raised his political consciousness which inspired the interest he has in politics today.

To help my dad, I had the idea of forming a savings club with my family members, but primarily for daddy. We started the club called *Griffin Family and Friends* and began meeting sometime around 1979. We alternated hosting meetings at various family member's homes. It was fun to get together with the family. I was lucky to grow up with spunky sisters. I looked forward to having all of them, Liz, Kat, Ersel, Gladys and brother Lawrence over to our home. My oldest Sister, Katherine (AKA Kat or Kittie) was regarded as feisty, energetic, and loved life. Kat pursued studies in computer science. She was stylish and well-dressed using her love for clothing as she worked at Hecht Company and got discounts for other family members. The next to the oldest sister Liz worked for the D'Alesandro family for 10 years as a cook and worked as a Dietician for the Baltimore City Public Schools. My sister Gladys (AKA Gla) completed coursework as a Dietary Manager at

Merganthaler Vocational High School. She was a faithful Cafeteria Manager at several Baltimore City schools. She managed a grocery store for her boyfriend Randy for many years and was lucky at hitting street numbers. My youngest sister Ersell was very smart, skipped three grades and graduated from Dunbar High School at the age of sixteen. I encouraged her to go to college but, I could not convince her even though I offered to finance furthering her education. She was the manager of a payment department for most of her career at NAC (which later became City Core).

Cardrienne would prepare a small meal and they'd bring their beer and favorite adult beverage. Sometimes their children would come over to fellowship as well. It was like a mini family reunion. We would start the evening with having a formal meeting including, established rules and bylaws. Afterwards though, we would have a good time catching up on what was going on with everyone. Each member contributed $10.00. In order for the money to grow we couldn't withdraw any of our savings for one year. Dad was to receive $10.00 a month. We had this savings club for many years but, it folded about 5 years ago. We hope to restart it with the next generation of family members.

We planned Griffin family and friends' reunions in which all were welcome. At our last reunion in 2015, we got together in Williamsburg, Virginia. My niece Robin and other family members did a fantastic job organizing and planning the reunion. It was a fun time that gave the children a chance to venture out to Busch Gardens and Water Country, but also a chance for us to honor our family who were no longer with us. It was the year after our middle daughter Debbie passed, so it was much needed time for us to be surrounded by the love of our family. Cardrienne planned a special Candle Light Tribute program. As part of the candle lighting, all family members present called out the name of a deceased family member. One by one, the names of my sisters: Elizabeth (Liz), Gladys, Katherine (Kat), and brother Richard, were called out loud; my daughter, Debbie; sister-in-law Aunt Julia; In-laws, Mama Lou and Pops, and many more. It touched a special place in the hearts of everyone who was there and perhaps not a dry eye in the room.

Four Candles (Author unknown)

Cardrienne started tribute.
The *first* candle represents our grief. The pain of losing you is intense.
It reminds us of the depth of our love for you.
Janelle:
This *second* candle represents our courage.
To confront our sorrow,
To comfort each other,
To Change our lives.
Michele:
This *third* candle we light in your memory.
For the times we laughed,
The times we cried.
The times we were angry with each other,
The silly things you did,
The caring and joy you gave us.
Jewel:
This fourth candle we light for our love.
We light this candle that your light will always shine.
We cherish the special place in our hearts
That will always be reserved for you.
We thank you for the gift
Your living brought to each of us.
We love you.
We remember you.

"Griff, where were you?" Cardrienne exclaimed calmly after looking around for me. I had to confess that I snuck off during this very important family event to go watch Serena play tennis on television. The bad part was that she lost that day. I suppose that was my punishment. A lesson learned - never miss a family event.

CHAPTER FOUR

STAND UP FOR WHAT YOU BELIEVE IN

"Most people know 'Griff' as a devoted husband and father. For me, he has always been 'Uncle Jim' and my most poignant example of a husband and father. While I remembered my own father from my earliest years, Uncle Jim became my living black male role model growing up. He is a true Renaissance man - a freedom fighter, entrepreneur, health, fitness and alternative medicine enthusiast."

Senator Jill P. Carter

TURNING BITTER EXPERIENCES INTO MEANINGFUL ONES:

I can recount facing racism a couple of times throughout my life. These twists and turns built my character, taught me to turn bitter experiences into meaningful ones, and raised my consciousness to fight for equal rights.

In 1958, Cardrienne and I moved in with my in-laws who were affectionately called 'Mama Lou' and 'Pops' at a single-family home on 3412 Batemen Avenue in West Baltimore. That was a bonus allowing us to save money for our own house. It felt like we were between a rock and a hard place though.

After working tirelessly for two years (1958-60) as a Physical Therapist (PT) at Montebella Hospital, I became disillusioned when I was passed over for a promotion as Senior PT position that I rightfully deserved. They promoted a Jewish female PT from out of state over me. The head of the department was an elderly white female physical therapist.

With the experience that I had in the department, I thought I deserved a promotion more than someone from the outside who did not have the credentials that I had. I was hurt and disappointed.

The silver lining was that shortly afterwards, a social worker friend (Sue Flowers), from our department, was able to help me get a scholarship to get my Masters of Science degree in Vocational Rehabilitation Counseling at Richmond Professional Institute (now called Virginia Commonwealth University) in Richmond, VA. While I pursued my degree (1960-1961), Cardrienne stayed with her parents in Baltimore.

Prior to finding a place to stay, I tried to eat in the cafeteria. However, I was informed by the Dean of the College that I couldn't eat there because the cafeteria was privately owned. Yet, I observed all white people eating in the cafeteria and no blacks. It made me feel insignificant in my own skin. Luckily, I found a room at Mrs. Lillie Thomas' house, who provided me with room and board (including food) for $40 a month.

FIGHTING FOR RACIAL EQUALITY:

The 1963 March on Washington occurred August 25, 1963, while I worked for the state. I didn't attend the March. I made excuses about not attending. At work the next day, a white co-worker asked me if I attended the march. I felt so guilty for not going to the march, I joined the Congress of Racial Equality (CORE) the next evening. For the first time in my life, I began to tackle racism head on.

Shortly after joining CORE, I met Walter P. Carter. Walter was very active working on the Gwynn Oak demonstrations. Walter had been meeting with the other CORE members in the 23 hundred block of West North Avenue in his sister's basement. She loaned out her basement for CORE to conduct our activities there. Walter was involved in a major way in attempting to desegregate Gwynn Oak Park.

Walter also played a major role in desegregating Ocean City. He corresponded with the leaders of Ocean City for several months, and literally forced them to desegregate Ocean City just by his letter writing, telephone calls, and threats to come down to Ocean City and demonstrate.

After Walter was sure that Ocean City was desegregated based on the leader's information to him, he took a trip with his wife (Joy) and their two daughters (Jill and Judy) to Ocean City to test out the realization that they had in fact desegregated. Upon coming back to Baltimore, he assured the other CORE members and myself that Ocean City was truly desegregated.

Within two to three months, I was elected President of the Baltimore chapter of CORE. My first assignment as President was meeting with the Superintendent of the U.S. Social Security Administration to discuss how to eradicate racial discrimination against African American men, primarily. Following the meeting, I felt increased confidence about confronting racism.

During my five years (1963-1968) as President in the Baltimore Chapter of CORE, CORE was active in confronting racial discrimination against public accommodations in bars, restaurants, hotels, houses, and apartment buildings. I was involved in many sit ins and protests and at times resulting in being arrested.

My oldest child, Cheryl, remembers hearing in school and coming home only to see on TV that her dad was arrested. I never spent more than a day in jail, but this did not deter me from continuing to fight for equal justice.

Walter and I, along with John Burleigh, and several other CORE members (white and black), were involved in a number of desegregation efforts in Baltimore, Maryland. We helped lead many demonstrations against bias in housing and public accommodations.

We desegregated Horizon House, Colmar Apartment in Painters Mills, Colonade Restaurant, Belvedere Towers, and the Vernon roller rink in Baltimore County. We demonstrated against the bars and nightclubs on Baltimore Street known as 'the block'.

Though we made many great strides, some of our efforts were met with opposition. For example, we were unsuccessful in desegregating a bar on Barns Street in East Baltimore and we didn't succeed at desegregating graveyards in and around Baltimore. However, we felt we really didn't want to desegregate them because we realized that if they didn't want to be near us in life, we didn't want to be nearby in death.

We were regarded as the anchor of hope for black people to gain our rightful place in a world that denied our existence. We set up an office on Eden and Gay street to do community organizing. Our office was staffed by Vivian, Pauline and a few others.

Shortly thereafter, we were approached by Dunbar High School students who claimed discrimination of their curriculum and inadequate instruction for their students. Our goal was to help them improve curriculum, ensure sufficient resources – such as more books, and transform Dunbar into a more competitive school in the area. In 1966, I received a Hall of Fame honor from my alma mater, Dunbar High School, for my civil rights involvement. I felt extremely proud and more empowered to continue in the struggle.

Looking back on these and other experiences makes me proud when I hear of how I may have impacted someone's life as a result of my struggles in the movement. Senator Jill P. Carter is one of the few people who I've had the honor of watching grow up and follow in the footsteps of her Dad (the late Walter P. Carter) fighting for equality in the black community. When Jill was asked how I've influenced her this is what she had to say.

Dear Uncle Jim:

Most people know you as 'Griff' as a devoted husband and father. For me, you have always been 'Uncle Jim' and my most poignant example of a husband and father. While I remembered my own father from my earliest years, Uncle Jim, you became my living black male role model growing up.

Your energy is placid and light with an unassuming, unimposing demeanor that exuded a quiet presence that created an air of ease in your home. So, even though there were many more people, the Griffin home was more mellow and relaxed than mine. Uncle Jim, you were always chill and if you were ever stressed or angry, I never saw it. What I saw was a true Renaissance man - a freedom fighter, entrepreneur, health, fitness and alternative medicine enthusiast.

Uncle Jim, you're the first truly open-minded person I've known - the embodiment of orthodox living and unorthodox thinking. While you assumed a traditional role of family man, you are not a traditional thinker. You are an explorer and more accepting of non-traditional thought than the mothers. I remember you showed me four eye exercises. You told me they hailed from the Chinese tradition and they would prevent bags and wrinkles. I was not more than 10 years old, but I did them religiously for years.

I learned about building black wealth by watching how enthusiastically you promoted and distributed the Bahamian diet and Amway, while running physical therapy as a primary business.

As a stalwart activist in the civil rights movement, which they just called 'the movement.' As a close friend of my father, I admired how both of you took direct action against discrimination. One of the frequently used tactics was to test rental policies, sometimes entering and sitting in apartment houses that refused to rent to blacks until removal by arrest was inevitable.

The mothers, Mom and Aunt Cardrienne, apprehensively awaited your return, hoping y'all would return home safely knowing death was possible. I saw how fathers had the courage and willingness to sacrifice their own lives for a greater cause - the realization of equality for all black people.

As an avid tennis player, you also combatted segregated tennis courts in the public parks, particularly the clay courts, that were eventually terminated when Blacks started using them. Perhaps when one engages in what should be normal activities knowing they can result in death, they became unflappable which is why I never saw you lose your cool when we children acted up even for things where there would be hell to pay by the mothers.

When I grew up and became a journalist, it meant a lot that you read my articles in the AFRO and would tell me they were well done. I was proud you actually read my articles. I have a profound respect and love for anyone that worked in the movement and with my dad. I have a profound appreciation for you, Uncle Jim, as a consistent calming and enterprising spirit throughout his life. Your interest and encouragement mattered and made me feel seen. Judy and I are eternally grateful for your example and guidance.

Senator Jill P. Carter

The Walk Out:

I worked at Crownsville State Hospital in Crownsville, MD for ten months. Shortly afterwards, I was recruited by Gil Ware of the State Human Relations Commission as an Equal Opportunity Assistant to the Maryland State Personnel Commission from 1965-1968.

After several months on the job, I went to a meeting where the 55th Governor of Maryland, Spiro Agnew was speaking to a number of human rights activists about not being as forceful as he thought they should have been about keeping rebel rousers in their places.

I looked around the room and saw many of my friends. I started out of the room and they followed me until the room was empty except the Governor. Several days later, a newspaper article featured Spiro Agnew chosen to be the person selected to be the Vice-Presidential running mate for the Republican ticket.

I may have had something to do with that appointment as a result of receiving national publicity about the walkout. Agnew later became the 39th Vice President of the United States (1969-1973).

AGAINST ALL ODDS:

> *"Jim and I would have many conversations about civil rights. I learned from him not only to talk about civil rights but to do something. Jim did not shy away from the problem. He was never satisfied and continued to fight for fair employment opportunities."*
> **Calvin Brown**

During my stint as Supervisor at the Maryland State Department of Education, Vocational Rehabilitation (1973-1978), it became apparent that I had to take action against all odds. A colleague and friend, Calvin Brown, described our experience there.

REFLECTIONS:

Jim is a serious individual but also could be funny. Our office was inside the pre-release center which was under the division of corrections. The agency provided lunch for $2.00. Jim would eat his lunch, other people's leftovers, especially the desserts. He never gained any weight and we started calling him the human garbage disposal.

We would have many conversations about civil rights. I learned from Jim not only to talk about civil rights but to do something. Jim did not shy away from the problem. Before Jim came to the agency, we were not fully committed to helping inmates.

With Jim's lead, we started a program to have inmates receive education and training outside of the prison walls. This was very difficult because the prison system is designed to keep you locked up and not to rehabilitate them. Jim was able to convince the prison authorities to allow inmates to receive services in the community. Jim reminds me of John Lewis, you see something, do something.

After the corrections program was closed down, Jim and I went to different offices. Jim saw discrimination in the agency. There were no blacks in management above supervisor one. With Jim, you see something, do something.

Action it was. We organized what was perceived as the Black Rehabilitation Administration. We sent a letter to the administration outlining our concerns. After several meetings with the administration, one of the Black supervisors was promoted to regional director. Jim was never satisfied and continued to fight for fair employment opportunities.

I decided to take several courses in real estate development and decided to start my own business. I talked to Jim about my idea and we decided to form a partnership. I wanted to make money, but Jim looked at the moral side of business: Are you making people's lives better? I never fully reached that moral issue, but I recognized business is more than just making money. Jim, thanks for making me a better person.

Calvin Brown

CHAPTER FIVE

PASS ON YOUR LEGACY

"When I was thirteen, my Uncle James enlisted me and my girlfriend Hazel to distribute flyers for an upcoming March. I knew my Uncle was very involved in CORE and the Civil Rights Movement but this small assignment reaffirmed it for me. He later paid us which was kind of a nice lesson in itself. My Aunt Liz kept a scrapbook of James' accomplishments, which included any newspaper articles."
LaFerne Johnson

STANDING UP FOR EQUALITY:

In reflecting on my experiences as the President of the Baltimore Chapter of the Congress of Racial Equality, CORE, I had become frustrated working through eliminating racial discrimination in Public accommodations, Housing, Employment and Education. I realized I needed to have a Full-Time President and a Fundraising arm of CORE, to be able to continue successfully in the struggle.

I shared this with Cardrienne and she agreed that a President of CORE, Full-Time, is a great idea and she would support me in coming up with a Fundraising arm of CORE, to allow us to be more successful in our pursuit of equal rights in Baltimore City.

In 1968, Cardrienne and I founded Woman Behind the Community, Inc. (WO-BE-CO) after first naming it Women Behind CORE. We decided that there was more work to be done in and for the communities of Baltimore. We selected charter members: Gwen Howard, Shirley Swafford, Carolyn Holmes, Vera Dorsey, Irene Reid, Mary Robinson, Marian Scarborough, Essie Sutton, and Regina Bernard. Cardrienne became the first President of WO-BE-CO. Her loyalty, wisdom and organizational skills united them to fulfill the many community projects and grow the organization. WO-BE-CO, Inc. is still in existence today after 50+ years of service to Baltimore Metropolitan Communities empowering women, children and families through health awareness, education, scholarships, employment development, civic engagement, and voter education.

Cardrienne enjoyed participating in many of WO-BE-CO's programs to serve the community and involved our children and grandchildren. I recall her taking Dominique, Jada and Coral to help her volunteer at the WO-BE-CO Dressing Room. The girls loved hanging with their grandmother there where they could help women, who may have experienced a hardship select clothing, jewelry, handbags, shoes, and accessories making it possible for them to start or go back to work. These women received job preparation and interview training from, and were referred by, the Mayor's Office of Employment Development.

The WO-BE-CO Dressing Room (the organization's signature program) located on the first floor, at 100 W. 23rd Street, has served more than 8,000 women over the years through community donations. WO-BE-CO has also mentored hundreds of young girls in Baltimore City. Cardrienne would volunteer with her WO-BE-CO sisters to mentor young girls at Edgewood Elementary School where this initiative is continuing.

CHAPTER SIX

GIVE BACK TO YOUR COMMUNITY

"My grandfather has taught me many things but the most important lesson I've learned from him is to be proud of who I am. He has always been so big on representing for African Americans and the black community and would hate it when I came to his house with straight hair. He always told me to be proud of who I am as a black girl and to embrace my natural curls. Almost two years ago, I cut my hair and actually he inspired it. I cut it because of damage but it's the best decision I've made in regard to my hair. I used to hate wearing my hair curly but, now I love rocking my Afro; so, thank you, for that Pop Pop: you're an inspiration to many."

Dominique Griffin (Granddaughter)

CHAMPION FIGHTER:

In 1968, after losing the election as National President of CORE, I felt somewhat relieved. I didn't want to continue struggling against the principle of desegregation as opposed to black power. The black power movement was being established and I didn't really want to stand in the way of the new wave.

Later that year, Baltimore's school system lacked leadership. I was honored to be appointed by the city's 42nd Mayor Thomas D'Alesandro, III (AKA 'Young Tommy') to the Baltimore School Board (succeeding Percy Bond who had retired). My acquaintance, Young Tommy, was regarded as 'a champion of civil rights' making considerable strides leading Baltimore from 1967-1971. He led the city during the 1968 riots, racial strife and strikes by city laborers, bus drivers and symphony musicians (The Baltimore Sun, 10/20/19). As a family man, he was also regarded for being kind to the poor and reaching out to help black people.

I served on the school board until 1974 under Mayor Donald Schaefer. One of the practices I fought to change was conducting public business in private sessions, which was illegal. I didn't have success challenging this practice until Attorney Larry Gibson was appointed to the Board and with the help of Betty Moss ("former reporter, editor and publisher of the Baltimore Afro-American newspaper") and Phillip Macht.

A very important event occurred in 1971 when Larry Gibson, Phillip Macht, Betty Moss, Buzzy Hettleman and I, traveled to Seattle, Washington, interviewed, and subsequently hired Dr. Roland Patterson as the 1st African American Superintendent of Baltimore City Public Schools. This was the first time we had any community involvement in appointing the superintendent.

When we traveled down from where we interviewed Dr. Patterson to the courthouse in the southern part of California, we saw Activist Angela Davis and her lawyer and one other person coming out of the courtroom. We greeted them and had a nice chat with them about what was going on with her case.

In 1971, the Baltimore School Board appointed Dr. Roland Patterson as Superintendent of Baltimore City Public Schools.

I, with the newly constituted board, worked tirelessly with Dr. Patterson to support several new initiatives.

While on the school board I fought to keep a Black man in charge of the Black history curriculum. The school system was attempting to remove many of our Black Books from the classroom.

I was instrumental in keeping Manchild in the Promise Land (Claude Brown), Native Son and Black Boy (Richard Wright) in the classroom. It was important that Black children read books that are relevant to our culture.

Dr. Patterson, assuming several major responsibilities (such as, balancing the school budget) took on the job with fervor. Under his impeccable leadership, nine independent school districts were created to improve learning; as well as a number of the new and progressive programs were instituted, such as establishment of a 'right to read' program and the requirement for substitute teachers to have a college degree.

Dr. Patterson did the job so well that the school budget was balanced with only about 200 dollars over the amount he was charged to work with. In my opinion, Mayor Schaefer and the City Council didn't like him doing the job successfully, so they felt he should be fired.

When Dr. Patterson was carrying out the programs that the school board had authorized, 'the powers to be' down in city hall became jealous of his popularity in the community, so we had a private meeting of the school board members earlier one afternoon.

Mayor Schaefer accused Dr. Patterson of misappropriating the Baltimore City School System funds. Dr. Patterson challenged Mayor Schaefer and sued the Mayor and City Hall Administration. The President of the School Board, Dr. Walton, called a private board meeting in order to fire Dr. Patterson for becoming a symbol of his people.

Larry Gibson, Betty Moss and I informed the community that Dr. Patterson was to be fired that evening. After the school board was convened, Dr. Walton attempted to fire Dr. Patterson by slamming the gravel on the desk and announcing his firing. I took the gavel out of his hand and took over the meeting. Dr. Patterson's position as Superintendent was saved for 9 more months. By taking over that meeting, this afforded Dr. Patterson another nine months to be superintendent in Baltimore. I was thrilled that we had saved his job - at least temporarily.

After saving Dr. Patterson's job, Mayor Schaefer replaced the school board President with Dr. Walter. Larry Gibson resigned from the board shortly afterwards. I was left alone on the board to fight our battles. Later that year, Mayor Schaefer, on December 31, 1974, sent a letter dismissing me from the school board. By that time, I had served two years over my appointed time.

HUSTLING TO MAKE ENDS MEET

Following Dr. Patterson being fired from his Superintendent-ship, it was necessary for him to maintain financial security. He and I set out on a fast and furious mission for survival. We went into several business ventures. We started a venture of selling black dolls donated to us from Watts, California after the riots in Watts. At that time, it was almost impossible to find black dolls and the ones you found had Caucasian features. Before we discovered these dolls, I painted ones black for my daughters so they would have dolls that looked like them. I remember Debbie cried when she discovered I had painted her favorite doll, Velvet, black. Admittedly, the paint that I used made her look unappealing. Needless to say, this venture became personal for me to allow my daughters and other black children an opportunity to have a reflection of themselves. We sold them throughout the Baltimore community. We went to various places to sell them including, Sparrows Point, where the workers would get paid every Wednesday and Thursday. We solicited not only the black dolls but, we had a raffle to raise money as well. I advertised the sale of the dolls through my various PT offices (at least 4 of them at that point) so for a while we had a pretty good venture going. We secured space appropriate to serve as a warehouse at Mondawmin Mall to store the dolls. I stopped selling Black dolls when it became difficult and expensive to get a shipment. We contacted the producers of the television show, Soul Train to help us market the sale and distribution of the dolls. Although they reached out, supply was limited and they were unable to help us.

Dr. Patterson and I also had a venture with Amway, where we didn't sell memberships but tried to build wealth using pyramid investing. We also started another creative venture known as a "car bar" which dispersed hot and cold drinks from automobiles. However, it wasn't profitable enough for me to keep this business. The car bar venture didn't last long and I began looking for a new opportunity to make more money. We didn't have the resources that we have available today to market the business to make it successful.

I felt good during those years working with Dr. Patterson doing creative business ventures to raise money for him and ensure he had sufficient salary to take care of his family. Eventually, Dr. Patterson was offered and settled on a job in New Jersey as an Assistant Superintendent of Education.

CHAPTER 7

TRAVEL THE WORLD

"What I learned most from Pop Pop is maintaining a close family dynamic. My family is extremely close and it started from my grandparents who were great examples. They exposed us to seeing the world through traveling and letting us know it's bigger than your city/state. Pop Pop has traveled all over the world and inspired me to want to travel. Being a family man and traveling are lessons learned from my grandfather that I will carry with me throughout my life."

Jay Threatt, Jr. (1st grandson)

I first started traveling overseas in 1977 with my wife Cardrienne. The NAACP sponsored a tour to get more African Americans exposed to the continent of Africa. We took advantage of this opportunity to visit and learn about Africa since it was so inexpensive. It was initially an investment of $200 per person for seven days including airfare and hotel. It ended up being $495 (with fees) but still it was a steal. We went to Dakar, Senegal. It was gratifying sleeping in a tent near the Atlantic Ocean.

We were so excited about what we learned that we took our four children the following year. We went to the following West African countries: Ghana, Liberia, Senegal, Sierra Leone, and Abidjan. We remember the people of Africa bartering for American goods. We were told to take blue jeans to exchange with the people of Africa because they were in high demand there. We exchanged our jeans and hair products for gold jewelry. The people were so nice treating us like family, although the food required some getting used to.

I remember getting off the plane in Dakar and Cardrienne was wearing a pink and green hat with her sorority, Alpha Kappa Alpha Alpha Sorority, Inc. (AKA) which caught the attention of the Ambassador of Dakar who was also an AKA. Their sisterhood connection was so strong and deeply rooted that even though we just met, she invited our entire family to her home for dinner. The Ambassador placed a big bowl of chicken, rice, and vegetables at the center of the table, and we all ate out of that bowl, sitting on the floor.

The most remarkable thing was taking my children on a tour to see where slaves were transported across the Atlantic Ocean and held in the 'door of no return'. In Liberia, we spent time hanging out with regular local people. We observed them working on their craft, making different clothing, slippers, etc. Abidjan was a little bit like a big city that was very advanced with all the amenities of home. By that time, our money was short so our family of six stayed in a motel in one room – little did we know until checking in that it was a prostitute hotel. It didn't stop me though from getting up for the free breakfast offered at the motel.

We spent three weeks in Africa. My wife and I were proud to give our children an awesome experience to be able to see how another culture lives. It was a memorable experience for my family to embellish on. Cardrienne encouraged our children to always keep a diary of all the places we visited as well as research its culture before leaving home. Africa is a beautiful place to visit that I hope my children will one day return and take their family.

Don't believe 'the hype' that you hear about Africa. It is the most rewarding trip you will ever experience. For African Americans, you should take your entire family so that you'll gain a greater sense of pride of who you are and from whence we've come. When we were in Africa, we met a young lady (Georgette) who wanted to come to the United States to finish school. She asked us for our phone number which we gave her. Little did we know that soon after arriving back home, Georgette called us from the airport and asked if we would help her. We picked her up and took her directly to the department store to get a winter coat, clothes and shoes since she came to America with no cold weather gear and no major necessities. What we thought would be a short visit, turned into a few months. Cardrienne and I were able to get Georgette in touch with her relatives in California, fly her there, and of course we helped her enroll into college.

We weren't financially wealthy, but we believed in giving our children real world experiences.

When Cheryl was sixteen years old, she remembers telling her friends our family went to Africa as well as several other places and some thought we were lucky. Our children and grandchildren have expressed how fortunate they feel that our family was afforded the luxury of traveling to faraway places. It was rare when they were young that other children their age traveled out of the country.

I'm pleased to have lived long enough to see my children and grandchildren traveling to many places around the world. My oldest grandson (Jay JR.) who plays pro basketball overseas, has traveled and/or played in numerous places including Germany, France, Hungry, Greece, Poland, Finland, Iceland and more. Whenever he returns home, he seems even more mature and confident which is why I think it's so important for people to travel and become exposed to various cultures and lifestyles. You learn more about yourself and others. It builds character, too. Cheryl and Jay enjoyed traveling to see both their sons basketball games including trips to Germany, France and Texas many times.

Our family travels also included Hawaii, California, Florida, Atlanta, etc. The only downside of traveling was we had to leave our pets. Malcolm especially had an affection for pets. You name it, we had it: a few dogs, hamster, bird, snake and now a cat. The most adored family dog was Chicka, who had beautiful black soft fur. I recall feeling saddened when we came home from California only to discover when we picked him up from the Vet that he dashed out, ran across the street, and had been hit by a car. Now that our children have their own families, they realize the cost to take a family on a vacation is enormous and better understand all the sacrifices Cardrienne and I made for our children. We didn't have a fancy car and never moved to a larger, nicer house. I still live in the same house today. I believe children may not remember all the material things you buy them but they will always remember the experiences.

My good friend Charles Robinson teases me about when Cardrienne and I took a family trip years ago and the plane was having maintenance trouble so when the pilot announced everyone had to get off, he said I jumped out of my seat and headed to the door so fast that I left them behind. It wasn't until I got to the door that I realized they were still seated. We still get a good chuckle out of that one.

In 1980, I was privileged as the only African American and the second group of American Physical Therapy Association (APTA) of American Physicians to travel to China. The highlight of the trip was walking the entire distance of the Great Wall of China. I was in awe that they actually had two walls: one for pedestrians and the other for automobiles. I brought my family back souvenirs and Cardrienne a 24-karet necklace, beautifully embellished with Chinese artistry that she cherished and wore every day from the moment she put it on.

CHAPTER EIGHT

BE YOUR OWN BOSS

*"Pop Pop and I worked together for 5 years and I learned
a lot working side by side with him. During this time
period of my life we became really close. I look up to him
in so many ways so everything he taught me I never took
for granted. Our one-on-one talks are when I learned the
most and I always got advice I needed. Pop Pop is my role
model and I hope to one day be a great family man and
entrepreneur as he is."*
Jamal Shannon (Grandson)

One thing you can say about me is I'm not afraid to take a risk.
Anytime the opportunity presented itself, I wasn't shy at trying a
new business venture. I probably pursued more businesses than your
average person. Sometimes I succeeded and sometimes I did not but at
least I never gave-up trying. I worked long and hard no matter what. I
continued to look for a business to sustain my family over time.

KANSAS CITY BARBEQUE

I remember being approached to be one of the investors of Kansas
City Barbeque selling barbeque spareribs and french fries. They

were short on funds to keep the business going. I was the sixteenth partner to get into the venture. I made an investment of roughly $2,000 and became an equal partner. Shortly after joining, I became very active in managing the business at North and Wolfe street. In order to increase our profit, we opened another location at Lanvale and Popular Grove. Our delicious smothering ribs drew widespread attention.

Cheryl who worked at the Popular Grove location remembers one exciting day, I got a call at the store, an order of barbeque was placed for Joe Jackson, father of the most popular teen iconic pop teen stars of the 70s, the Jackson 5, who were in Baltimore for a concert. When I went to deliver the food to their hotel, I boldly asked if I could bring my girls back to meet the Jackson 5. Soon after arriving home to share the good news with my daughters, our home was instantly filled with yelling and screaming preteens from the 'Griffin girls Jackson fan club'. The Jackson 5 picture that hung in their bedroom was coming to life in their imagination. Cheryl and Debbie, who loved the Jackson 5, were excited. They hurriedly got dressed and put on long white boots and brown 'hot pants' (as they called them) with matching shirts and a scarf around their neck. Cheryl happened to be sporting a large afro indicative of the 1970's trend. You couldn't tell them they weren't cute! The girls fussed over who was the cutest to them, and which Jackson they were going to marry. Jewel, who adored Tito Jackson, pouted because she was too young to go. Cardrienne stayed home with Jewel and Malcolm. By the time we arrived at the hotel there were a few other girls swarming around, and the Jacksons were all in their rooms. Disappointed, the girls only got a quick glance at Jermaine just quick enough for him to autograph their crinkly blue paper. It was enough to put a smile on their faces and the highlight of their summer. Cheryl must have slept with that autograph under her pillow until she went to college.

Unfortunately, even though the food was a hit, management of the business was filled with challenges. There was a robbery at the Popular Grove location as well as poor management at the Lanvale location. I hired one of my nephews to manage the second location to try to revive it. We looked for other ways to increase profits by selling more Barbeque Ribs. We joined the City Fair downtown and set up a booth one weekend from noon until dark. The Monday morning after the fair, I discovered we should have made more profit than what was accounted for. These were the defining moments that led me to get out of this business.

MY HOUSING BUSINESS VENTURE:

In 1975, Calvin Brown and I were Vocational Rehabilitation Counselors for Maryland State and had become friends. We decided to fix up old homes. My sister, Katherine wanted to sell her house after her husband (Roscoe Wharton) passed away. We bought the house and rented it after renovating into three units.

A short time later, we involved a third partner in our newly formed partnership by purchasing his parents' home at 1218 N. Bond Street, which was vacant and in need of repair. We didn't realize how much rehab work was required until the demolition was started. At that point, we hired my nephews: Garry and Jerryl Brown, plus Gil Stephenson to complete the demolition.

We moved to another venture at 1616 Druid Hill Avenue and quickly realized we needed more money to rehab it. We called an additional friend to become limited partners as investors only. We were successful in bringing in five limited partners at $2,000 each or $10,000. We continued to purchase dilapidated homes, renovated them, and rented them into one, two and three apartment units. Eventually, we bought out our limited partners.

The largest venture we started was a house at 2501 W. North Avenue where it required a bank loan of $30,000. We used the $30,000 to renovate the house into 6 apartment units. The next loan for $10,000 was for 2505 W. North Avenue. We made that into three apartments. After 25 years of managing properties, we decided to sell all of our real estate.

GRIFFIN ASSOCIATES, P.A.:

I recall the day when I had enough of working for someone else. My life took a turning point starting in 1979 when I worked for about two years as a Physical Therapist (PT) employed by a group of doctors at Park Heights office. I became frustrated working under the management of the doctors. My desire to open my own practice grew more and more each day.

When I approached the doctors to explore opening my own practice, they kept avoiding me for months. Finally, I just walked out and decided to quit and then they called me back and met with me to set up a meeting. As a result, Griffin Associates, PA was formed.

With only a few pieces of equipment, I started to build my private practice. I became the first African American to own a private physical therapy business in Baltimore.

My desire was to train up a generation of minority physical therapists by creating career opportunities for them in a profession that they were not traditionally exposed to. I paid one year of tuition for nine Howard University students in exchange for one year of guaranteed employment post-graduation. Unfortunately, the majority of students did not fulfill their year of work commitment or pay back their tuition as agreed. One of the students, Billy Anderson, was the exception. He was a dedicated and loyal employee of Griffin Associates for thirteen years. Another student with whom I had the privilege of mentoring was William Garrett, who humbly expressed his gratitude and what he learned from working with me as follows:

"Mr. Griffin has had a tremendous impact on my life that continues to this day. We first met in the fall of 1988 when he

was seeking out young African American Physical Therapists (which were rare at that time) that he could mentor in order to carry on what he started in the profession. His goals were to not only provide quality care, but to be a healthcare advocate for the underserved population, while owning your own practice. I was immediately sold and felt very comfortable because he led by example.

There was another therapist (Vernise Burs) that believed in his vision and we both took a leap of faith and entered into business with Mr. Griffin in the spring of 1989 and formed Burs, Garrett & Griffin Physical Therapy. Mr. Griffin began to transition into retirement in 1993 and the practice later became Burs & Garrett Physical Therapy Services. With his guidance, both practices were very successful, thus fulfilling his goals. As a result of our professional relationship, he instilled the confidence in me to be a vocal advocate for the healthcare rights of minorities and to join other organizations that fought for the same cause. I've also gotten involved with other mentoring organizations as a way to give back to the community like he gave so much to me.

On a personal and social level, Mr. Griffin and I enjoy playing tennis, which has further strengthened our bond and has allowed me to spend additional time with him. He has introduced me to many of his personal friends that I now have a great relationship with. He has taught me how to maintain a humble spirit, even in times of adversity and the key to getting whatever it is in life that you want which is getting along with everyone, even if you do not agree with them."
William Garrett.

I started an organization called CHARM for minority Physical and Occupational Therapists in the Baltimore/Washington area where therapists could discuss their concerns in the field of therapy. After a few years, Griffin Associates, PT expanded and added a

2nd office, Jai Medical Center. I also opened a 4th office briefly 3 days a week at 810 Park Avenue. It truly became a family business.

While Cheryl, like all my children in some way or another, worked at Griffin Associates, she was most captivated by it. At the age of 12, she started working with me in middle school at Park Heights Medical Center as a receptionist. Later she worked as a PT Aide in my offices. At that time, she didn't show any interest in physical therapy. She attended Virginia State University majoring in Mathematics. While at VSU, she got a job working at Hopewell Hospital as a PT Aide for one year. That exposed her to a different aspect of therapy in a hospital setting. Soon after, Cheryl developed an interest in Physical Therapy following in my footsteps. I never encouraged her to pursue the profession, so I was surprised when she called me to tell me she was interested. In fact, unbeknownst to me, I could have discouraged her from going into the field because I was afraid by that time the requirements had become too stringent. Nonetheless, she didn't listen to me and I'm glad she didn't. She later graduated with a B.S. in Mathematics, applied and got excepted at Howard University's PT school. Cheryl is passionate about helping others in the community as a Licensed Physical Therapist where she resides in Richmond, Virginia. For years, she would drive back and forth helping me out in the business.

My wife retired from the school system after 17 years and became the Vice President of the business and worked 13 years with Griffin Associates. My wife managed the office and was able to improve the overall business. My oldest sister (Kat) worked closely with her at Jai Medical Center and they helped the business to expand. My niece Michele (our Godchild), aka Mickie was a PTA. She also worked for me as well as many other family members were employed with Griffin Associates. It was truly a family business which was important to me.

As I reflect back on Griffin Associates, that business was really the impetus behind my life's passion for helping others. I took great pride in taking care of people of all ages and walks of life. I treated a range of patients requiring physical therapy from athletes to people suffering from muscular disorders to rehabilitation from automobile accidents. I also found joy in nurturing all my staff and treating them like family. A young lady, Chanel Mosby, pursuing an internship at Griffin Associates became like another daughter to us. Here's a personal reflection from Chanel.

"During my senior year in high school, I became a student intern at Griffin Associates, P.A. I was young, it was my first time working in an office setting and I was extremely nervous. I wanted to make a positive impression and perform well. All of my worries disappeared after the first morning. Everyone was warm and welcoming and seemed eager to help me. I looked forward to going to the office each day because I always left having learned something new and motivated to do better the next day.

Over time, my professional skills developed and my confidence increased. I began using the skills that I was learning at Griffin Associates while working on the weekends in a department store. As a result, I was promoted to the Head Cashier. I observed the caring way that Mr. and Mrs. Griffin interacted with family, staff members and patients. I marveled at how they lead a successful business and devoted their time to organizations that helped others in the community all while maintaining family as the number one priority. I learned many valuable lessons from Mr. and Mrs. Griffin about leadership, charity, priorities, and compassion. Those lessons have served me well in my professional and personal life.

My internship came to an end during the final quarter of the school year. I looked forward to graduating and finding full time employment. Although I did well in high school, I never considered attending college because I never enjoyed school. However, Mr. and Mrs. Griffin strongly encouraged me to register for college because they knew the value of education. They recognized something in me that I didn't see in myself.

I took their advice and I've never regretted it. I worked part time at Griffin Associates while studying to become an Elementary Education teacher. I took my role as a classroom teacher, seriously. Every student needed someone to believe in them and help them to prepare for success beyond the classroom just as Mr. and Mrs. Griffin believed in me.

I've always felt extremely blessed to have positive role models in my life like Mrs. and Mrs. Griffin. My students benefited from what I learned from them about work ethic, compassion and patience. The leadership skills that I learned from Mr. and Mrs. Griffin helped when I became a school principal. I was able to collaborate with other educators to develop strategic academic plans that were implemented school-wide. I worked to build positive relationships with others in the community by helping to facilitate various outreach and charitable efforts. Those actions often led to students receiving essential resources such as dental care, eyeglasses, housing, food and clothing. Ultimately, I strived to be the positive role model, encouraging and caring adult to my students that Mr. and Mrs. Griffin have always been to me.

Somewhere between the first morning of my internship and the end of my senior year of high school, Mr. and Mrs. Griffin became my "bonus parents" and I gained an entire bonus family. I am forever grateful that throughout all of my life's joys, challenges, peaks and valleys, God saw fit to bless me with them." **Chanel Mosby.**

Owning a business is hard work, but very rewarding. You work harder for yourself than other people, but I wouldn't have traded it for the world. It felt good to be self-sufficient and to be able to take care of my family and help others in the community. I had to learn self-discipline though. I couldn't sleep good at night until I paid my bills. Although we didn't live lavishly, I made sure my family got to enjoy some delicacies in life. I was able to take my entire family of six on yearly vacations and pay for my children's college education.

I considered having reached my business goal of securing a good life for my family which to me meant achieving personal success. One day, I realized that I was mentally and physically burned out from the long 10+ hour days, non-stop from office to office. I decided after 25 years of operating the business that it was time to retire.

Upon my retirement, I sold the business to my niece Mikie, PTA and Janice Bowie, P.T. and a former co-worker. Mikie had been a loyal and dedicated employee for many years. I was happy to keep the business in the family.

CHAPTER NINE

HELP OTHERS IN NEED

"I learned so much from my grandfather through observing his actions and listening to his stories. I appreciate every lesson he's taught me, some without even realizing it. I learned discipline through seeing him commit to a pescatarian diet for as long I've known him. I learned resilience from hearing him speak about how he overcame racial barriers. I learned professionalism by hearing about how he was able to open up businesses and own properties throughout the city. The most important lesson that my grandfather taught me is selflessness. I will never forget coming over his house and taking down all of the plaques he received for giving back to the black community. He gave back to his household as well as staying happily married for over 50 years and being a direct influence on the lives of each of his children."

Thank you, Pop Pop, I will always carry them with me, Jada Shannon

A Dream Deferred:

On March 16, 1984, myself, Melvin Fossett, Dave Montgomery, Charles Simmons and Roderick Richardson crossed over the burning sands into the Omega Pi Chapter of Omega Psi Phi Fraternity. We persevered through weeks of sometimes embarrassing, sometimes agonizing, sometimes difficult times. I felt rather proud having gone through that experience at 52 years old while running a business at the same time. It was also gratifying that I was able to finish what I was unable to in college, for financial reasons.

I was recruited by Dr. Charles Simmons, President of Sojourner Douglass College and one of my line brothers in Omega to join the Board of Directors in 1985. Under the leadership of Dr. Simmons, Sojourner Douglas had a forty-one-year history of providing educational opportunities to traditionally nontraditional adults in the community. The college operated out of six fully accredited locations in the state of Maryland and a branch in the Bahamas. Experiential learning was the concept utilized across the college system to assist the students to become self-sufficient through education, jobs, applied research, training, and community organizing. This clinical concept was an outgrowth of the college's mission of self-determination and afrocentrism.

Shortly after becoming a board member, I learned the college was in financial debt primarily with the federal government and state of Maryland. Part of the reason the college was in debt was their inability to pay state and federal taxes due to low student enrollment based in part from the federal educational change in guidelines. After the college couldn't pay the aforementioned debt, the Middle States Atlantic Association withdrew our accreditation. I was disheartened that Sojourner Douglas closed its doors on June 30, 2015. One of the proudest moments of my life was when I got to witness my grandson Jamal Shannon earn his bachelor's degree from Sojourner Douglas.

During my first year as an Omega man, I served on the social action committee under Lester Buster. During my second year, I assumed the Chairmanship. Mr. Samuel Billips called Billy Hice, who is an Omega, and his Physical Education department, and myself to help some at risk Walbrook High School male students. Billy and I tried to hold the first-year meeting with the boys with little success.

We went and assembled a larger social action committee consisting primarily of Carlton Gordon, Antonio Carpenter, Dwayne White, Charles Simmons, Paul Mountain, Mickey Giles, Eric West, Riley Coakey. We started mentoring sessions every other Saturday at the Omega Fraternity Center; as well as, on Tuesdays and Thursdays, in various schools including Walbrook, Carver, Edmonson, Matthew Henson Elementary, Greenspring Middle, Pohaten Middle school.

On most Saturdays, my Omega brother Jestus Johnson and his wife participated with their son and daughter for our social action mentoring and giving out Thanksgiving food giveaways at our fraternity house. Much like my wife and I, their mentoring efforts made a positive impact on the lives of young people in the Baltimore community. As positive role models, it manifested into Jestus's son being active in his high school, serving as president of a black youth group, playing football and attending college.

One of our mentoring sessions also involved inviting guest speakers to share life lessons to the boys. I invited my frat bother Carlton Gordan's wife Francis, a registered Nurse, who did a lecture for the boys on the negative consequences of unprotected pre-marital sex such as, how they could contract venereal diseases and damage their immune system.

In another mentoring session, I invited my neighbor across the street, Charles Ford, also known as 'Bubba', to talk with our mentees about their experiences with taking a non-traditional path and finding success as an entrepreneur. The takeaway from his pep talk with the boys was that you can still be successful and find meaningful employment without a college degree but it's much more difficult. Thus, it is important to enroll in a structural trade school or certificate program. He worked hard at Pep Boys for eighteen years and faced challenges taking that long to become one of their black supervisors. Over time, Bubba realized that it was better for him to get all the fruits of his labor by working for himself. After many attempts at applying for a loan, he obtained enough capital to start his own car repair shop (Bubba's) in West Baltimore.

The committee started taking the mentees on two college tours per year to Historically Black Colleges and Universities (HBCUs) such as, Lincoln University, Chainey University, University of Maryland Eastern Shore, Morgan State University, South Carolina State, Coppin State University, and Hampton University. We also visited other institutions of interest such as, the Smithsonian and Frederick Douglas museum in Annapolis, MD.

In addition to college tours, the social action committee took very meaningful trips like an overnight stay at a hotel in downtown Baltimore. We brought the boys to spend the night at the home of Omega brother, Cecil Robbison, who lived in Baltimore county. Our fellowship with the boys was a wholesome weekend filled with delicious breakfasts and suppers, and watching movies in his very elaborate television room, and playing games.

Another field trip was taking the boys (mentees) on a retreat. On the retreat, we were not allowed to have televisions or radios. In seclusion away from city life, it enabled just the social action brothers and mentees to interact with each other and discuss meaningful topics relevant to helping them grow from boys to men. Mel Faucet wasn't an active member of the social action committee, but he, Tony and his wife, made very nice contributions towards the efforts of the committee.

My wife's cousin Frenzela Credle was one of our social action committee supporters, especially for our college tours for our mentees and the coed Historically Black College & University tours. She would often meet us at the buses and pray for our safe journey to and from the colleges. Frenzella would also provide financial help to the social action committee.

Concurrent with the college tours sponsored by Omega Psi Phi, Cardrienne and I along with other alumni members of the Inter-Alumni Council of Black Colleges and Universities, resumed college tours to various colleges including, Johnson C. Smith, North Carolina Central, Morris Brown and South Carolina State University. During the tour to Morris Brown, we pointed out to the students on the tour that Cardrienne's Grandfather and Great Uncle were Past Presidents of the college. I believe this stunned them.

Through the 16-18 years as chairman of the social action committee, I was awarded four Omega prestigious awards: Omega Man of the Year, Founders Award, Bridge Builder and Superior Service Award.

"In the words of Carlton Gordon, my Omega Psi Phi fraternity bother: I met Jim in the fall of 1986 through our graduate chapter Pi Omega in Baltimore, Md. While Jim was Chair, I was Co-Chairman of the Principal Achievers committee, this is where our friendship began. Jim was a healthy eater and eventually I followed him and gave up eating red meat and pork which I have continued to do. He had the whole committee getting away from eating red meat. Jim was consistent about his health and those around him. He remained very active and would participate in senior Olympics and played tennis until the end of 2019. He never had any health concerns.

Jim and I began traveling together on many occasions, watching him being honored for his many well deserved civil rights achievements, neighborhood, and many other local involvements. We had the opportunity to travel with our spouses on fraternity trips but later it blossomed to us traveling with just us four on vacations. This is where our bond had the opportunity to grow even stronger. Jim became my big brother.

We shared successes and failures, buying and selling real estate, and the horror stories of being landlords. We shared many stories and Jim was my confidant.

It is not often that life affords us the opportunity to have as an endeared friend, a father, leader, role model, a man of such integrity, vision, and compassion as I have witnessed. Jim has the admiration and respect of countless individuals whose lives he has touched, impressed and engaged. I often run into acquaintances that ask, "how is Jim?" Students that are now grown continue to ask about him. For he has taught many young boys lifelong lessons. Jim's accomplishments, honors and recognition would be a challenge for the average individual. Yet, in spite of all his esteem recognitions, awards and accolades, Jim remains a humble and caring man. My friend!!!" **Carlton Gordon.**

We didn't do a formal evaluation of our program, but were able to locate three of the Principal Achievers: <u>Dontee Jones</u>, graduated from Southwestern High School and went to community college studying Business Administration. He did odd jobs in the community and slowly built up enough work to start his own contracting business. He is married with two children and doing well. <u>Shalik Fulton</u> graduated from Carver High School and started working with Councilman Nick Mosby. When Councilman Mosby was elected to a Senate position, Shalik became one of the Assistants to States Attorney Marilyn Mosby where he is currently working. <u>Damon Williams</u> graduated from Carver High School and is successfully employed and happily married with one child. He is another good example of employing what he learned from the mentoring program that helped guide him on the right path in life. If life has afforded me nothing else, it has given me the chance to help someone else along the way. This is the way I have tried to live my life, taught my children, and encouraged others to do likewise.

CHAPTER 10

FACE YOUR FEARS

*"I learned that courage was not the absence of fear,
but the triumph over it. The brave man is not the one
who does not feel afraid, but he who conquers that
fear." Nelson Mandela*

I remember the long drives Cardrienne and I had back and forth
to the hospital to visit our middle daughter, Debbie. Watching
her suffer from breast cancer was probably worse than the pain we
endured when we had to let her go. Her husband Dean was always
by her side. He took Debbie to her appointments, read a lot of her
treatments, advocating with her doctors to make sure she received
special care.

Cardrienne was so brave. I admired her strength and courage. She
kept everything inside but I knew it was troubling her. To me,
it was unspeakable, and undeniably more than words could ever
express. Men are naturally taught not to cry because it appears
to be a sign of weakness and to stay strong for our women and
children. But I could not hold back my tears when I got the call to
come to the hospice on that dreary 5th day of April 2014.

Days leading up to that, through all hours of the night and morning, our family surrounded her bedside day in and day out of the hospital. Dean beside her; children Jamal and Jada; her brother Malcolm; both sisters: Cheryl who came with her husband Jay, Sr. from Richmond, Virginia and Jewel along with her daughter Coral. It was like this over the course of five years during her many stays in and out of GBMC Hospital and St. Agnes Hospital, only a longer list of family and close friends.

Many of her sorority sisters of Alpha Kappa Alpha Sorority, Inc. (AKA) especially in her graduate chapter (Rho Xi Omega) where she actively served, would alternate bringing her home cooked meals to her home. Debbie received frequent calls, visits, and special gifts from a wide spectrum of friends from all walks of life, ranging from Western High School to Virginia State University college friends; friends who worked with her at the U.S. Department of Health and Human Services where she worked nearby, and many more. This outpouring of love was no surprise to us because Debbie was the kind of person who would do anything for everyone.

Debbie's fun-loving spirit, much like her Mom's, was what kept us grounded. Through all her chemotherapy treatments and doctor appointments, she never complained. Nor did she let cancer defeat her. Instead, she resolved with more vigor to make the most of every opportunity. Her courage and strength taught us all to embrace life and live it to the fullest.

Family meant everything to her, not to mention friends. We would tease her that every week she would come home with a new best friend. Everyone loved her easy-going, warm personality. Debbie was a lot like Cardrienne – she was a spitting image of her inside and out in that regard. It is ironic that they were both diagnosed in the same year (2009) with breast cancer but, neither one of them let that stop them from living

Debbie was 'the glue that held us all together'. With excitement, she would organize all the details for every family event. From her children (Jamal's football games to Jada's dance recitals and fashion shows) to all her siblings. All of us would get a call telling us where we needed to be, what time we should be there, and sometimes what we should wear.

She would get so excited whenever we would go on family outings. It did not matter to her whether it was only 15 minutes or hours away, she would be the first one ready. On long trips, she would pack her clothes a week before and call every day to tell us something new she had purchased to add in the suitcase.

I recall us going to my grandson's, Jay, Jr and Jarvis, basketball games at Delaware State University and the University of Delaware. They both received full college scholarships. Debbie was so proud of them and enjoyed organizing the family and friends' attendance at their games. We took many road trips to watch them play. Filled with excitement, our family would all sit together and cheer them on.

Debbie was everyone's cheerleader. Cheering from the football field for Jamal when he was in Little League to Jada's dance performances. She made sure the auditorium was packed full of family and friends. I was amazed at how she would get several of her friends to come out in support of her children too. Two special occasions come to mind when we were filled with astonishment for her daughter Jada as the leading role of Maria in the Baltimore City Nutcracker and as Director of Carver Center for Arts and Technology's fashion show.

Debbie had gotten really sick, started to deteriorate, and lost a lot of weight, but she was determined to ride up with the family to Jarvis's championship basketball game at the University of Delaware (UD). I remember UD was tied and with a few minutes left in the game, Jarvis determined to win for his aunt knowing deep down inside it may have been her last time seeing him play, he pushed himself on the court, stole the ball and made a shot to tie the game with seconds on the clock to win the game. It was extra special because they won their first CAA championship game, with Jarvis, as most valuable player, dedicating his winning trophy to Debbie. She was so excited.

It made me proud to see Debbie, and all our children, follow in our footsteps. What I learned most from being a father is the importance of being present in your children's lives. I made sure no matter how busy I was over the years, whether it was running my businesses or serving in the community, I was there for all my four children's and grandchildren's major events. Watching my children grow up, observing how the value of family and community has transferred to them in their lives, made me realize that it's true - children learn more by what they see rather than what you say.

When my mind drifts back to when Debbie was transported to the hospice facility and I see Debbie unconscious, she is lying in the bed motionless, unable to speak, but I knew she felt our presence. I hated seeing her like this. I wanted more than anything for her to wake up and for this to be just a bad dream. Being at the hospice was the longest day ever in my life. When Cheryl arrived from Richmond, VA, Debbie turned and looked up in her direction as if to say "now that my oldest sister is here, all the family is here, now I can rest." The nurse informed our family that Debbie was transitioning, but it would be another day and everyone should go home, but Cheryl and Jamal stayed there by her side in the final hours.

After it got late, Cardrienne and I went home. My heart would skip a beat with anxiety every time the phone would ring. Worried, wondering if it is the day I'd receive the dreaded news I never wanted to hear. Lowe and behold, it was around 4:00 a.m. on April 5th when Cheryl called Cardrienne and I, and my heart dropped. She called other family, too. When we arrived, we discovered Debbie took her final breath with her son Jamal holding her hand. Our family poured in and comforted each other. I have somehow blocked that day out of my mind. It is too painful to talk about.

In the months that followed, as our coping mechanism, Cardrienne and I would listen to the sermon multiple times by Rev. Jamal Bryant, who delivered the sermon at Debbie's funeral. It lifted our spirits and reminded us that Debbie had fulfilled her purpose.

Thoughts of how much she was well-loved, warmed our hearts as evidenced by hundreds of her sorority sisters pouring in the sanctuary at Bethel A.M.E. Church where her homegoing was held. We were touched by the long line and massive number of beautiful ladies of AKA adorned in their white dresses for Debbie's 'Ivy Beyond the Wall' service, a ritual of the sorority. Her blood sisters and sorority sisters (Cheryl and Jewel) and Cardrienne were overcome with emotion at that time.

My fraternity brother Rev. Ronald Hankins, who lived up the street and had his own church [Trinity Presbyterian Church] around the corner, gave us words of comfort and encouragement at the service and would stop by to talk with us heart-to-heart in person.

As time went on, I watched Cardrienne be a pillar of strength for our family. If it had not been for her, I would not have been able to get through this nightmare. I was going through the motions, but life didn't quite seem the same. It was a void that no one or nothing could fill. Yet, through it all, Cardrienne would tell us to keep our heads up. Cardrienne was truly one of a kind. Catching us off guard, you would never know what Cardrienne would say. She had a unique way of making all of us laugh even on those hopeless, gloomy days.

Cardrienne even formed a special bond with Debbie's close friends who were like our adopted daughters. They would call or write, and she'd give them words of encouragement or simply fill their souls with laughter. I remember one of Debbie's good friends, Sharronne, who often called to check on my wife, but wound-up feeling overwhelmed with emotion, so Cardrienne ended up cheering her up instead. Well, one day Sharonne told her that she didn't feel up to coming to a family event. Cardrienne told her: "Now, you know you're going to have to come so just put on your big girl panties."

After one long year, our family attended church together at Empowerment Temple. We were invited by her God Father Charles Robinson. We had to draw on our faith together as a family. Rev. Jamal Bryant preached a dynamic sermon that was a pillar of strength for us to carry on. I wore my necklace with Debbie's picture around my neck which I never remove.

Worshipping at Empowerment Temple with Charles Robinson

CHAPTER 11

KEEP YOUR HEAD UP

"Who could find a virtuous woman? for her price is far above rubies. The heart of her husband doth safely trust in her, so that he shall have no need of spoil"
Proverbs 3:10

Four years later it was déjà vu as Malcolm and I walked in the dining room and noticed Cardrienne was moving slow, unable to formulate her words. I was afraid. We called the ambulance, who loaded her on the stretcher and headed to St. Agnes. Jewel and Cheryl met us and rushed to her side too.

There our family gathered again, pouring out our love in this ole too familiar hospital room, but, this time it was Big Mama we attended to. She had a mild stroke. I felt helpless. I was a Licensed Physical Therapist and it seemed there was nothing that I could do to help the love of my life.

The girls stayed overnight with her in the hospital, sleeping on the chair, as they did with their sister, Debbie. Cardrienne couldn't get out the bed without our help. When she improved, the hospital transferred her to the University of Maryland Rehabilitation Institute at Woodlawn. Of course, Cardrienne didn't like the idea of going there. She wanted to go home. She tried to get the ambulance driver to make a detour and take her home.

The facility took good care of her, but I knew Cardrienne didn't want to be there. She was astute when the speech doctor came to evaluate her. Cardrienne made sure to answer all the right questions accurately and precisely so they'd release her. She joked with the nurses and physical therapist too. Cardrienne kept her antics going as long as she could. After an overnight stay though, she became unresponsive again and was rushed back to the hospital.

Malcolm, Cheryl, Jewel and I were in the Emergency Room for hours by Cardrienne's side. We were worried about her, but she was still her playful self, which at least eased our mind a bit. Eventually, they admitted Cardrienne, moving her to a private room and it was later determined she had another stroke. This time it was more severe.

My wife quietly slipped out of my hands and into an unconscious state. We waited for what seemed endless while doctors ran tests to determine what could be done. It was a blessing that Debbie's close friend Lamonde was a nurse and advised us on what doctors were telling us. They moved Cardrienne to intensive care and now I had to be braver than ever especially for my children and grandchildren.

Members of WO-BE-CO AKA sorority sisters, modern grannies, and member of the Links, came by her side expressing their sincere well wishes and prayers. Other close friends and family including, Malcom's son Sean didn't want to leave his grandmother's side, Chanel, Larry, Bill and Wanda Brown flooded her room spilling over to the hallway. We exceeded the maximum limit of visitors, but the hospital staff was so accommodating, they let us pamper her - even brought us extra pillows/blankets at night to help make us more comfortable when we stayed by her bedside all night. We didn't leave her side. We formed a circle around her bed and prayed. We played her favorite music by Luther Vandross, yet, Cardrienne remained unconscious.

After a few days, the doctors told us there was nothing else they could do, and moved her from Intensive Care to Hospice Care. At that point, the number of visitors was limited. Our immediate family remained constantly there by her side. Malcolm, Dominique, Cheryl, Jewel and Coral took turns being by her side. Her club members WO-BE-CO, close friends and neighbors came by to visit Cardrienne. She was so popular that we started a guest book. Going back and forth to the hospice became a routine. Each day, going in and out of the hospital, we had to face our fear of the inevitable. One day although still unable to speak, she perked up and we were able to take pictures with her. It lifted all our spirits. Cheryl (who we call "Dr. Threatt" of the family) spent the night and was there alone with Cardrienne when she took her last breath.

My life came to a screeching halt on the 15th day of April 2018. It was the day my world crumbled. My heart skipped a beat when I discovered Cardrienne's no longer beat. In those last moments, time stood still. Our family sat motionless in disbelief. Saying goodbye to the love of my life, and the rock of our family, was the hardest thing I, or any of us, had to do.

The days following that dreadful day are a blur. It was another time in our family saga when we had to keep our head up. Cheryl and Jewel pulled the arrangements together and with the outpouring of support from family and friends, we had a beautiful service and tribute to Cardrienne at the historic Bethel African Methodist Episcopal Church located on Druid Hill Avenue in Baltimore city. When I walked in the antique smell of the 235+ year-old church still lingered in the air, stain glass windows, and pipe organ left intact from its original state, bringing back memories of where we were married nearly sixty years ago when our journey began. As I leaned in to keep my composure, Melody Harris, a college friend of my oldest daughter stepped to the podium and delivered an inspiring poetic rendition and account of Cardrienne's legacy.

Tall structures left behind are marvelous indeed/ like the pyramids of ancient Africa, and immortal monuments of our greatest leaders.

BUT.....when up close and in person the direct recipients of what has been carved and branded on the hearts and minds of those who were loved and left behind in order that they may perform even greater and divinely illuminate task in the kingdom of God.

Then a legacy is etched and fixed into the souls of others who will tell the true story about the precious and cherished work, the impact that was mounted and erected here on earth continuing to beat like the drums of our beloved ancestors, a living pulse that somehow flows from one generation to the next, and the next.

I know of such a legacy up close and in person. There is a story of a lovely lady who raised three little girls of her own, and unlike Mrs. Brady the fictitious Hollywood character of the 70s. This lady had a much deeper call on her life.

Now I don't know what God whispered into her innocent ears as a young lady but judging from the fruit that sits before us she must have obeyed in her spirit the direction of the Lord. Along with her beloved King they planted produced and harvested a fine crop. Behold the evidence that this woman of God followed a divine direction.

One of the most telling of her obedience is that in 1953 she answered the call completed her pledge requirements and was initiated into what was then what is now, and what will forever be until the end of time as we know it the first and greatest sorority of the Divine 9. Absolutely no offense to those of our beloved sisters who carry any other name and colors.

In 1953 at Virginia State College this woman received her pearls and was proudly initiated into Alpha Kappa Alpha Sorority, Incorporated Alpha Epsilon Chapter, and I must say she revived her pearls and hit the floor running carrying out the mission of the original founders of 1908 and she did not stop until the good Lord called her to take rest in heaven. May I pause to get an Amen from my Sorors.

While I will not share the ongoing details of her impressive contributions within our sorority leaving that up to those who saw her in her specific functions, I will say that you know something is divinely orchestrated when the offspring follows a mother's footsteps into the same place of post-secondary studies and seeks and gains entry into the same sisterhood, continues to carry on the mission of that sisterhood, and prepares the way for the next to join them. All active and all working to promote high scholastic, ethical standards, promote unity, improve social stature and interest in college life, and service to mankind. If this is not a perfect example of legacy, I don't know what is.

You do not have to be a member of our sorority to witness this legacy you just have to know these ladies up close and personal. Like their mother and grandmother, they are beautiful, courageous, leaders, friends, loving, change agents, smart, loyal, fun, trendy and fashion conscious, who speaks their minds, and does what they speak. One, my line sister can even be a little bossy. (No names).

All the Sorors who got to know her through her daughter were also benefactors of the legacy through her tutelage, for yet better not be in her presence lacking the representation of an AKA.

I can't help but think about our beloved Debbie who left us only a short time ago. Her line name Hitler. So, she was bossy too. But, I think mostly of what we can't possibly and completely imagine, that in a twinkling moment in time the continued legacy beyond this life into the next, a place in paradise where She waited beyond the river for her mother to join her in glory. There is no greater legacy.

Cardrienne Griffin 1953 AKA,
Virginia State University

Cheryl Griffin- Threatt, 1981, AKA,
Virginia State University

Debbie Griffin Shannon, 1982, AKA,
Virginia State University

Jewel Griffin Linzey, 1986, AKA,
Virginia State University

Jada Shannon 2017, AKA,
North Carolina A& T

Continue the good work of Cardrienne Griffin 1953

Alpha Kappa Alpha, Incorporated

That poetry spoke to the consciousness of my soul, for it awakened in me the quiet place that could not be disturbed. Now sitting back hearing about Cardrienne's legacy and beautiful spirit that exhibited a strong sense of purposefulness, influenced her children to follow in her footsteps by attending her alma mater, VSU, and in turn trail blazed a beloved family legacy of all her daughters being initiated into the same chapter of Alpha Kappa Alpha Sorority, Inc. and later one of her granddaughters (Jada) at North Carolina A&T, was profound. It spoke volumes about the positive influence she had on our four children, eight grandchildren, and two great-grandchildren.

I was no longer numb from the pain but filled with pride, mulling over how much an impression Cardrienne left not only on Cheryl, Debbie, Jewel and Malcolm, but on the lives of many. Another one of the highlights of that heartbreaking day was when my favorite songstress Miriam W. McKinney blessed us with a beautiful rendition of a favorite song of Cardrienne's: "His Eye Is On The Sparrow" which warmed my heart. Cardrienne's Godchild (Cheryl Ann) joined us from North Carolina recounting fond stories: '70 years of loving memories' having met Cardrienne as a young girl who sixteen years her elder looked up to her with admiration. Their friendship blossomed and sustained throughout their lives. It was touching as Cheryl Ann shared how she was the Candlelight girl in our wedding professing that we were one of the happiest and gracious couples she'd known, illustrating the time when we bought her first car.

The ladies of Women Behind the Community, Inc. gave a 'Rites of Passage' service honoring Cardrienne as Co-Founder and for her long enduring service to the organization. Other leaders from various organizations she served gave homage to her service in the community. Immediately following the service, the repast was held at the Ivy Center where Cardrienne served as President of the Epsilon Omega chapter of AKA for four years, in many leadership capacities, and would frequently work at the Ivy Center dedicating her time serving meals to seniors as part of the "Eating Together" program.

When all was said and done, it was a rebirth for me and all of us. Cardrienne's passing meant I had to learn how to take care of myself. I had to figure out how to cook more than just oatmeal. I grew lonely with the emptiness of her lively presence that once lit up each room. I began to miss her signature dishes such as, chicken salad, mac and cheese, and soulful collard greens Cardrienne made just right for me to perfection! Only she knew how to cook my greens long enough but not overcooked to maintain all the nutrients. Cheryl and Jewel started practicing her signature greens plus other dishes and stepped up making the holiday family meals. There was a little tension at first but in time they managed to alternate hosting holiday meals at their homes with ease. It's been a joy to see them take over and also teach my granddaughters

Dominique, Jada, and Coral, dishes too. Malcolm has been helping to contribute towards the meals which makes me happy.

I'm thankful to have a good support system that has made this transition more doable. For a while, I continued to work at PB Health, and my neighbor Monica would drive me to/from work after my children insisted that I should not drive anymore. I was resistant to that idea early on but accepted this as a natural progression of getting older.

One of Cheryl's good friends and college roommate (Lori, with help sometimes from her sister Sherri, Jewel's freshman college roommate) would bring me home cooked meals once a week. From time to time, Cheryl and Jewel make me meals. Jewel and Coral take me grocery shopping every other week. Malcolm also picks up food for us and does handwork around the house. I'm glad he lives with me to give me some companionship, and it has strengthened our father-son bond.

After nearly 60 years of marriage, I think back to what made our relationship so special. As I reflect back to many blissful years together, I can definitely say that Cardrienne always supported me immensely. Cardrienne was the quintessential essence of a virtuous woman.

She always had nice home cooked meals waiting for me after a long day at the office and made sure that our family sat down at the dinner table to eat together like clockwork every night at 6:00 pm. No television was allowed. She proclaimed this as 'family time' and would go around the table to find out how everyone's day was. It was important to her that we'd all share stories of our day with one another. She would have plenty of stories to share about when she was a Senior Teacher.

After dinner, she would love to play the piano. I was impressed that she didn't know how to read music but could play by memorizing the notes. It was typical for us to gather in the living room to play games with the children. We'd also listen to R&B music on our record player.

Cardrienne and I both worked full time and were involved in the community through our own separate organizations, plus we supported each other's events too. We gave each other enough space to develop our own interests, yet we would join forces together to support one another's worthy social causes. This made our marriage unique. It's important to let your significant other spread his/her own wings independently and apart from you to ensure both of you are happy. If only one of you is actively involved and doing good things in the community it means the other will feel envious or neglected.

However, if both of you are fulfilling your purpose, and making a difference, it will equate to both individual's self-fulfillment and inner happiness. The cliche "don't depend on someone else for your happiness" manifests itself in marriage.

Not only should you have your own interests, but you should support each other's too! Now I'm not saying Cardrienne had to go play tennis with me. Sure, if that was her thing that would have been nice. It definitely was not. I'm not even sure if she ever picked up a tennis racket. All jokes aside, I really did not expect her to. That is my passion, not hers.

We had many other things in common. For instance, we both loved to travel and enjoyed getting away from it all at least once a year -- sometimes with just the two of us and other times with the children. So, finding mutual interests, hobbies or commonality is important in relationships. Sometimes it comes naturally and other times it may not, which means that you will have to do some exploring.

I'll give you an example of how Cardrienne and I supported each other. Cardrienne was active in several civic organizations including, Bethel AME Church, Alpha Kappa Alpha Sorority, Inc.,

(Epsilon Omega chapter), Baltimore Chapter of the Links, WO-BE-CO, Inc., Spokettes, MG Modern Grannies, and life member of NAACP. I, too, was active in Omega Psi Phi Fraternity, Johnson C. Smith Alumni Association, and Sojourner Douglass Board. One of the organizations we were both involved in and attended meetings together was our community Fairmount Neighborhood Association.

Since both of us worked full time and actively served in various community organizations, you think that meant we wouldn't have time for each other or the children. Not to brag, but, we didn't miss a beat. We managed to still give one another the time and attention we both needed by going to each other's organization's events. For instance, if the AKAs had a dance, I was there with Cardrienne. Likewise, if the Omega's had a event, she would go with me. We were 'social butterflies.' We definitely made a lot of friends in Baltimore.

Now sometimes, the events may not be as lively, but it was fun just to go out together and socialize with other couples. Cardrienne really enjoyed getting a new outfit to the formal events. I'd wear my same tuxedo just change the bow tie or tie occasionally. The children would get a kick out of taking pictures of us, sending us off as if we were going on a prom date. Cardrienne fit perfectly with women from all walks of life and society. Everyone loved her and enjoyed being around her. She would crack jokes and have you laughing all the time. When it came to getting things done though, she took care of business. Well organized and like Emily Post, Cardrienne planned and organized all three of our daughters' dream weddings. They were all elaborate and attended by hundreds of people.

It wasn't always about fun and games though as she worked tirelessly in those organizations, doing work in the community. Cardrienne was dedicated and hard working in her organizations. In her retirement, she enjoyed helping others in the community. Faithfully, she volunteered set days/times each week whether it was serving seniors meals as part of the AKA Eating Together program, or helping women going back to work obtain donated professional attire at the WO-BE-CO Dressing Room or mentoring fifth grade girls at WO-BE-CO's adopted schools such as, Gwynns Fall Elementary or Edgewood Elementary.

Her schedule was full, yet she took care of home, family and herself, and she made it look effortless. She had a routine of sleeping until 10:00 a.m. making sure she informed all her friends and associates not to call her before that time. Also, she arranged her schedule such that she'd have time to go grocery shopping and have dinner ready by 6:00 p.m. She carved out time on Fridays to get her hair done and of course go to the children or grandchildren events. She didn't miss any of them and made sure I didn't either. She would sit in her chair at night, organizing her time and events, and wrote down everything in a weekly planner/calendar to keep on track.

It's important that young people not only make family their top priority, but also serve in the community.

I am a proud JCSU graduate. This is significant cause we believed that our HBCU's build character and produce strong, confident professionals. Cardrienne and I have always supported our HBCU's financially and encouraged our family to do the same.

We have a strong multi-generational tradition of HBCU graduates in our family -- Mama Lou - Morris Brown College, Pops - Paine College, myself - JSCU Cardrienne -Shaw University and Virginia State University, Julia - Shaw University, Cheryl - VSU and Howard University, Jay Sr. - VSU, Debbie and Jewel - VSU and MSU, Jada - NCA&T, Kevin- NCCU, Jay Jr. - Delaware State Univ. , Michele - Coppin State College, Quinn- Bowie State and Robbin - Howard University. The tradition is continuing with the next generation.

CHAPTER 12

JUICE UP, GET FIT, AND BE HAPPY

"Pop Pop has inspired me to be conscious about what I put in my body such as the food I eat, what fruits and vegetables I consume as well as fluids. To see him still in great shape and health moving around as well as he does is nothing short of amazing! He has also taught me a great deal about what it means to be a family and how family should always support each other. Pop pop was always there for me at every special moment, big games and Graduation and from that I've learned what it means to be a family and how we celebrate each other's accomplishments like they are our own!" **Jarvis Threatt (Grandson)**

Over the years, I pride myself on being a pescetarian. I choose not to eat red meat. Mainly, I eat fish and vegetables. I've grown to eat various types of fish (from salmon and tilapia to catfish), veggie burgers, turkey burgers and acquired the taste for a host of other foods.

I didn't impose my beliefs on my family but sure tried to get this point across to them. According to the late Civil Rights, Vegetarian Activist and Comedian Dick Gregory *"It's cool to be healthy."* I essentially showed them a healthy lifestyle by my example of eating and exercising right.

I did not stop there. I also introduced my family to some of my veggie drinks that I'd make secretly hoping they would still somehow adopt my way of life. I enjoyed experimenting with different ingredients like carrots, celery, and cabbage for instance. When they found out what I put in my smoothies, they frowned upon it. It was a hard sell. Plus, they were too indoctrinated to the poor food habits of society. I'm afraid that fast food and eating out has brainwashed the younger generation. Though I admit, desserts are my weakness and an occasional veggie burger from Burger King suits me just fine. I do believe though that because of my active and healthy lifestyle is the reason why I don't have any medical problems other than just the normal issues that come with aging, such as arthritis.

Even though I haven't been able to sway my family over to my lifestyle, I still served as an 'advocate' to others. Some of my frat brothers were intrigued. They invited me to give demonstrations on how to juice.

I was an ardent tennis player, too. Up until I was 87, I managed to fit in playing tennis once a week. I deemed it important, especially with my rigorous schedule of managing business or career while meeting the demands of balancing taking care of my family and serving the community. I would play once a week with Dr. Harold Ramsey, William Garrett, Mickey Fields, and Steve Ward. We all shared a passion for the game of tennis a number of years. Their friendship is essential to the soul.

I occasionally still try to hit the tennis ball when I can but, my frail knees have inhibited me from playing competitively. Instead, I adopted a ritual of watching tennis matches on television – especially rooting for my favorites (Venus and Serina). That is one of the joys of retirement that I don't have to miss any of the games.

Years earlier, I introduced my niece (Laferne Nole) to the game of tennis. I took pride in taking her under my wings and coaching her.

"We really started to have fun when James introduced me to my love of tennis. I really didn't know how patient he was until years later when I started taking lessons. James again, knowing I was taking lessons, invited me to join his Wednesday evening tennis games and I became one of the regulars. We had a great time playing and it was always really fun when James and I teamed up. James was the same, not criticizing but giving me pointers and encouraging me. We made it to our Wednesday games through rain, snow and ice. I think one night, Aunt Cardrienne talked us out of going because the weather was too bad. As I played and watched more tennis, we started calling each other about the games. We discuss the matches and the players and James would fill me in on their backgrounds. Of course, we always root for all the Black players, but we enjoy watching all the good players, especially the Williams Sisters."
Laferne Nole

During the 2020 national COVID-19 pandemic, I started walking around my neighborhood once a day to keep me in shape and maintain my balance. I have come to realize that another part of one's health is also about finding your happy place and doing what you love.

Our neighborhood is nestled within a serene five-street wooded southwest Baltimore neighborhood, backing the breathtaking Gwynns Falls Trail. Baltimore Sun editor [Barbara Haddock Taylor] described the neighborhood as 'a well-kept secret'. According to Fairmount's current President (Leslie Imes), one of the joys of living in Fairmount is "the pleasure of knowing most of our neighbors and watching them grow up and look out for one another.'

This is a neighborhood of many pioneering and reputable black professionals who made an impact in the Baltimore community. There are long-time residents (such as, Dorsey, Arnold Hayes, Head, Howard, Payne, Reeves, Shelton) who were staples in the community and well known for their contributions as educators, lawyers, judges, nurses, politicians, etc. Many people may not know that Fairmount was home to the late Wesley N. Shelton, a black pharmacist who co-owned four drugstores throughout the city; the late Charles H. Dorsey, Jr. (Agnes), the first black attorney to serve and chair Maryland's State Board of Law Examiners and Executive Director of Maryland's Legal Aid Bureau, Inc. who was well regarded for increasing access to legal services for low-income and disadvantaged people. Dorsey, a father of eight children, all of whom have successful professions.

We were also honored to live near other pioneers: the late honorable Judge Joseph C. Howard, the first African American elected as judge for the Baltimore City Supreme Bench and the first African American to serve on the bench as United States District Judge of the United States District Court for the District of Maryland (appointed by former President Jimmy Carter). Fifth District Councilman Norman Reeves who was followed by his wife, Iris Reeves formally as the Fifth District Councilwoman. Longtime resident and community enthusiast Ms. Georgia Payne, a former nurse now in her 90s was believed to have created the first dialysis unit in Baltimore. I was the first black physical therapist who went into private practice in Baltimore. I am thrilled to have mentored and trained countless physical therapy students, encouraging them in their academic and professional pursuits.

Walking around the neighborhood that I've lived in for over 59+ years, with the sun glistening over me, I reflect on how happy Cardrienne and I were that we raised our children in a black family-oriented community. Not only did everybody know each other's names, but we looked out for each other too. A feeling of sadness suddenly came upon me. This is different than how I see things now. I hardly ever see children playing outside at all anymore.

Unlike the good ole days when streets were filled with the joyful noise of children playing games. I'd come home from work often to several children in the neighborhood playing baseball in the alley beside our home. Our home was also the hangout spot for Jewel and Malcolm's friends, often playing basketball or other games on the patio. Those days seem long gone. Children nowadays are fixed to their cell phones, X-boxes, and other electronic devices, nestled at home for the most part with little interaction with others. I wonder if the pandemic exacerbates this phenomenon.

I thought about how during the 1960s', Cardrienne and I were leaders in the community at the height of the civil rights movement that was the impetus behind the vision of Women Behind the Community, Inc. (a, spinoff of my stint as President of the Baltimore Chapter of CORE). Many neighbors like Judge Howard and his wife (Gwendolyn) joined us in the fight for equal housing, education, employment opportunities, and fair pay. Our home was one of the breeding grounds for formulating ideas and plans to make changes in the community. Neighbors would congregate in our living and dining room or basement for meetings. My daughter Jewel fondly remembers a time when Cardrienne and I joined the teacher strike for higher pay at her school (Edgewood Elementary School) where all three of her siblings attended school.

At the heart of Fairmount Park are lots of fond memories where we invited neighbors over for dance programs in our living rooms, games, and holiday festivities, too. Our next door neighbors, the Tocci's, would also host Halloween Parties. My oldest daughter (Cheryl) remembers when on any given day, the neighborhood children would have car washes, bake sales, play hopscotch, and dodge ball together. Everyone would look forward to our annual neighborhood picnics that brought all the families together. Years ago, when the Howards were residents, the picnic was held at their home which had a beautiful swimming pool for all to enjoy.

Our Children enjoyed hanging out with their friends in the neighborhood. Malcolm was often at the Matthew's home hanging with Darion and also at the Franklin's with Eric. He also hung out with several of the guys around here (including, Nick, Junior, and Alex) and continues to this day. Jewel liked to play mainly with Leslie. Cheryl and Debbie would hang out with Nina and Angelo as well as, primarily Jocelyn and Allison Head across the street. Those friendships have sustained long beyond their humble beginnings.

As I peruse through the streets, taking slow strides, I awaken my consciousness that over the years, our neighborhood has struggled to get residents involved. Due primarily to gentrification, many younger families moved to the suburbs and the neighborhood is made up mainly of seniors. Nowadays, it is often difficult to get residents involved in the neighborhood. It is my hope that one day we can get back to the way things used to be. Those were the good ole days.

CHAPTER 13

LIFE'S GREATEST TREASURES

Life's greatest treasures are about celebrating one's proudest moments. To me, it is not the plaques on the walls or the degrees I've earned, but the lives I've touched along the way that mean the most to me. Being a husband, father and grandfather is the most profound and highest honor as a man. Sharing and giving to others above myself on my journey has felt good. I loved, I hurt, I succeeded, I failed, I laughed, I cried, I lost, but most of all, I gave. I gave the best part of me to bring out the best part in others. I could have shared a thousand endless stories of ups and downs, and more bumps in the road of life along the way. It was my vision though to share lessons I've learned, as a result, of many experiences deeply rooted in my upbringing that molded and shaped me into who I am and what I stand for as a black man in America. These lessons are really from you, for you and because of you. It is because of you I am who I am.

As I near the end of this book, I want to devote this chapter to recounting my proudest moments that amaze me about my eight grandchildren and two great-grandchildren. My life as a Grandfather began with making a mad dash on 95 south from Maryland to Virginia. What fascinated me most on becoming a grandparent for the first time was discovering it meant you no longer have the control you once had. This eye-opening phenomenon was fine with me especially since it didn't come with any responsibility: we could arrive on our child's doorstep with one suitcase and leave empty handed.

Our first grandson, Jay, Jr. arrived on a hot summer August day, and four years later his brother Jarvis, to my oldest daughter (Cheryl) and son-in-law (Jay, Sr.) who were VSU college sweethearts. Jay Sr. played basketball at VSU and coached his sons to be well-disciplined and skilled players. He was a point guard and taught both his boys to be ultimate point guards. Jay Jr. Was awarded the National Collegiate Athletic Association NCAA Mens Division 1 statistical Champion for steals. In 2010 2.8 steals per game and 2012, 3.0 steals per game. Holds the assist record at DSU. Jarvis was 2011 Parade all American in High School and Player of the year in 2010. They both attended college on full scholarships. Jarvis won the 2015 NBA G League Slam Dunk Contest. Cardrienne and I enjoyed going to their basketball games over the years marveling at their swiftness and invincible talent. Their basement is filled with trophies and accolades adorning the wall, resembling a hall of fame.

My second grandson, Jamal, arrived on my birthday. He was my 'surprise' birthday present from Debbie one 11th day in March. I got a call from Debbie one night when we were at a hotel in downtown Baltimore celebrating my birthday and she called to tell us to come right away because she had a present for me. I casually told her, "thanks and congratulations, but we would be there tomorrow" because we had paid too much for the hotel room. Jewel, her surrogate labor coach, had walked up and down the hospital that night for seemingly hours, was there by her sister's side. They could not believe we didn't come running like we usually did and teased us for years. Although Jamal has a more loquacious, wild and crazy temperament than me, now in his 30's, he has recently developed the same entrepreneurial passion, drive and determination as me when I was his age. I'm thrilled that he's recently started his own part-time Hedge Hunter's landscaping business which makes me proud. His son Riley, born one year after his mom's passing has been the light in his life. They are like two peas in a pod always talking and joking non-stop. Let me interject, Jamal and Jarvis, are the two comedians of the family. They make me laugh until my stomach hurts.

I must brag a little that my granddaughters are all pretty, talented, and smart. The oldest, Jasmine, born and raised in Richmond, VA and now based in Atlanta, is a rap artist who writes and records her own music. Jada, who lost her mom in her last year of high school persevered by staying on the honor role, enrolled in, and graduated Magna Cum Laude from North Carolina A&T, got a full scholarship to obtain her Masters Degree at Michigan State and is now working at one of the top accounting firms in Atlanta. Dominique, a graduate of Stevenson University, is a hard worker and dedicated in her computer profession. My youngest granddaughter, Coral, a high school student, has a caring heart and sweet spirit helping me out each week with a mom (Jewel) to get groceries and even cooks meals for me, too. She is also on the honor role. Jada, Dominique and Coral are all gifted in dance. It's been a joy to see them dance beautifully in various genres of dance (including, ballet, modern, jazz, hip hop, African) performing in various concerts over the years especially in leading/solo roles. Both Coral, of Baltimore Dance Tech (BDT) and Jada (BDT alumni) auditioned and were selected varying years for the leading ballet role of Maria in the Baltimore City Nutcracker. Dominque mastered command of the stage in modern and hip hop at Western High School (WHS) and as part of the WHS Alumni Dance team.

Our family welcomed Jarvis and Destiny's son Jeremiah, my second great-grandson in 2019. I wish Cardrienne was alive to see him. She would have been as fascinated by him as I am. Cheryl's mother- in- law, Grace Threatt, simply adores Jeremiah, holding and smiling at him all day. I think he is everyone's beacon of hope, with so many tears shed from the loss of our loved ones (Grace and I had in common that we both lost a daughter) and with the void Cardrienne leaves in my life, Jeremiah gives us that spark that we needed. Watching Jeremiah is fascinating, full of personality like his dad, and at 18 months, he looks as tall as a three-year old. I believe he might be destined as the next Threatt basketball player to carry on their legacy.

The year 2020, I was thrilled when my grandson Sean (Malcolm's son) graduated from Edmonson High School. Until Covid, he was able to work. Sean's mom worked tirelessly with Malcolm to hold a drive-by graduation celebration and cookout that brought him to tears, surrounded by family and friends. I only wish Cardrienne (who everyone affectionately called Big Mama) could have been there to see him graduate. I know she was smiling down on him. He loved his grandmother and enjoyed visiting with us every other weekend. Now, he and I have bonded.

If you're reading this book, it's likely that you were apart of my life in some kind of way and you helped shape me into who I am, or ever hope to be. Forgive me, that I didn't recall every name on the pages of this book. I had so many sleepless nights trying to remember all the people, places and events over the span of my lifetime. Surely, I left out so many family, friends, or ordinary people (like my patients, co-workers, neighbors and others) who although not mentioned were really an extraordinary part of me. Blame it on my mind and not my heart. Life owes me nothing more because I know that I've been incredibly blessed by countless people too many to name. If you learn nothing else from me, it is my hope that you learn that in my personal dictionary "selflessness" is a four-letter word for the word "give"! Always remember, we are not put here for ourselves, but to give the best of ourselves for someone else.

CHAPTER 14

THE POWER OF MY JOURNEY, MY WAY

Each careful step along the byway
And more, much more than this, I did it my way
Yes, there were times, I'm sure you knew
When I bit off more than I could chew
But through it all, when there was doubt
I ate it up and spit it out
I faced it all and I stood tall and did it my way
I've loved, I've laughed and cried
I've had my fill, my share of losing
And now, as tears subside
I find it all so amusing
To think I did all that
And may I say, not in a shy way
Oh, no, oh, no, not me, I did it my way

Excerpts from 'I Did It My Way', Frank Sanatra

As I reflect on my 89 years of life, I can say I did it, *My Way*. Growing up a young black boy on the East side of Baltimore in the 1930's, who lived through poverty, racism, segregation, oppression but always had the determination to want to do better. What made

90

me strive to go to college, pursue a Masters Degree, and start a business, I do not know exactly. The more I read and observed what was going on in my community, I just knew that I had to find the strength and courage to be a better man. I had the privilege of being exposed to positive role models and the remarkable experience of a college football scholarship that led me to an incredible nurturing HBCU in the south that changed the trajectory of my life.

When I think back to the way things were when I was growing up and the way they are today, I see some things haven't changed much. The divisions that surfaced from the oppression of Trayvon Martin, George Floyd, and countless other incidences that took innocent lives of black men (and women) too soon, reminded me that racism still exists in this country, and we're still divided. The 'Black Lives Matter' movement that surfaced, revealed there truly is 'Two Americas'.

Yet, in this infinite recycling of pain and oppression, I never thought I would live to see a black man become President of the U.S. The pride I felt when Barack Obama was sworn in as our 44th President in 2014 is something I will never forget. And now to witness another milestone, our Vice President is a black woman is remarkable. Kamala Harris, a member of Alpha Kappa Alpha Sorority, Inc. and a graduate of an HBCU, Howard University gives me hope that things may be going in the right direction. It gives me pride that our V.P. belongs to the same sorority as my wife (Cardrienne), all three daughters (Cheryl, Debbie, Jewel) granddaughter (Jada), niece Michele Morton, sister-in-law (the late Julia) and her granddaughter, Taylor , and Taylors mom Gloria, the late Sujette Fountain Crank, former South Atlantic Regional Director, maternal cousins Frenzela Credle and Denise Greenfield.

The love and strength of family has sustained me throughout my lifetime. Cardrienne was the glue that kept our family together while I pursued my career, community service, and life in politics. She was always able to make sure the children were provided for, attended all their activities, Vice President of Griffin Associates,

P.A., as well as my partner in assisting with all my organizations, while she too worked in the community. Together, my wife and I earned over 35 community awards. We had a stable home with lots of love.

We worked hard to pay for our children to attend college and trade schools without taking student loans, bought each of them a car, and helped them with other major purchases whenever they needed us. Likewise, we gave to anyone else in need. This is not to boast, but to share that putting our family and friends above ourselves, has been far more rewarding than anything else in life.

We were never financially wealthy, but we had plenty of wealth. I never purchased a new car for myself, and material things do not matter to me. What mattered most was making a difference in someone else's life, whether it was my own children, extended family, or a stranger.

My life crumbled when I lost my rock, my wife, the woman I loved for 60+ yrs. Seeing her in the hospital after having a stroke was the worst day of my life. I remember thinking, "how do I go on without my Cardrienne?" It was reliving the pain I felt from losing my middle daughter, Debbie, which left a void that was unlike anything I ever experienced. Watching how brave she was as she battled breast cancer was remarkable. She never complained and continued to work and care for her family the entire 5 years as she fought that dreadful disease. It gave rise to the message of 'live life to the fullest'.

Still living in the same three-story house for over 60 years has brought stability. We chose to give our children experiences instead of a lot of material things. Now don't get me wrong, they like material things, but they are not measured by things, but were taught to give more than to receive. We showed them how to love, give back to their communities and that family is always first. No amount of money could replace those values. Our home is filled with so many memories. Everywhere in my house I feel the presence of my darling wife and daughter. They are always in my heart as I miss them dearly. The loneliness I feel without my two angels is real. However, I continue to push on because that's what they would want me to do. My Cardrienne was the strongest woman I ever met. She taught our son and daughters to be just as strong. When I feel the emptiness in this house without her, the memories keep me going. My other children, family and friends are always around and see that everything is taken care of for me. My son lives with me and we have gotten closer since their passing.

In 2021, who would have thought we would be living through a pandemic. With the social distance implications of Covid 19 affecting us all, it has forced me to reflect back over my life and emerge feeling even more blessed to have known true love as a husband, father, grandfather, great grandfather, uncle, brother, friend, and mentor. Thankful for all the lessons I learned throughout my life, and grateful that I left many lessons and a legacy for those whose path I crossed. Grateful that I have been able to observe first hand that my children learned from the examples we set. Knowing they will carry on our legacy with their children is all I could hope for. I thank God for allowing me to enjoy a life well lived by doing it my way. My favorite singer is Frank Sinatra and the words to this song, "My Way," will always play in my mind.

JAMES M. GRIFFIN

TRIBUTES

The following tributes are lessons learned written from my family and friends that parallel the trajectory of passing down my legacy.

Thirty-two plus years ago, Griff trusted me to marry and love his daughter always. I hope after all these years, you see that I am a man of my word. We've always had a good relationship, with me looking at you as a father figure and giving you the respect you deserve, but you would always say, "I'm just one of the guys." Hearing that from you let me know that no conversation was off limits with you. You are a great example of what a caring husband and family man should be. Thanks for your trust. **Jay Threatt, Sr. (Son-in-law)**

One of the things that's always said is, "Don't watch what someone says, watch what they do." Over the years, I've admired the way Mr. Griffin carried himself as a family man. He's a man who is always there for his family. Mr. Griffin has always been a person who's been involved in working in the community from the civil rights days to the present. I think the trait that I admire the most is the belief he has in other people. It takes a certain type of person to see the good in others that can be so easily overlooked by most. **Dean Shannon (Son-in-law)**

My Uncle James had an influence on my life at an age. Being a Carpentry major at Lake Clifton High School soon after graduation our paths crossed on a business level. After seeing some wall framing I had done at home he wanted to know if I could do the same thing on a larger scale. Things we learn in school from Teachers and Books do not compare to actual hands-on work in the field. After a few years of renovating and rehabbing houses for my uncle and his partner not only did I build my confidence but, I honed my skills to a professional level. After years of working as a Contractor, I developed plumbing and electrical skills. Needless to say, without my uncle giving me a chance to not only practice and hone my skills, It gave me a chance to improve my knowledge of the contracting business and develop new skills along the way. Experience is the best teacher. Thanks Uncle Jim. - **Forever Grateful, Jerryl Brown**

Uncle Jimmy looked out for me while I was growing up. Obviously, growing up in a single-parent household in the '60s was not the best, but I survived with the help of family. I am thankful for the fond memories my Mom (the late Dr. Julia Davidson) and I shared with Uncle Jimmy over the years. No matter the reason or the need, he has always found a way to assist first and ask questions afterward. His unselfishness modeled for me how to be a loving father and teacher. -**Kevin Davison (Nephew)**

Uncle Jimmy has truly been an inspiration and role model who we will always and forever love and respect. Filling in as practically our own grandfather, Uncle Jimmy has taught and shared with us so much about life. The level of humility he exudes and the knowledge he has shared over the years will be forever engraved. He has taught us how the love of veggies, fruits, and fish can do the body well, how standing up for what you believe regardless of the consequences (civil rights movement) can and will only make it easier for our next generation, and how love, dedication, respect, and regular communication with your spouse and family helps establish the foundation for generations to come. **Love you always, Taylor and Kyle Davidson**

An African proverb says that 'When an old man dies a library burns'. My uncle is still around, Iam listening and continuously receiving wisdom and knowledge from his library in order to continue his legacy. I hear his voice, at times when I want to quit this journey of activism, telling me to "keep going -don't stop". Whenever I get tired or need a clear, patient and understanding voice, I sit and talk with him. He always makes me feel like I can conquer the entire world.

Thank You for blessing me with your presence in my life, as I take this baton, running on the path you laid out for me and so many others. One day you ask me who I look up to. My heart and soul look up to you. You are one of my greatest inspirations. Thank you for teaching me and always being there. I hope I make you proud. **Love You, Crystal (Great niece)**

Every time I've ever made time to sit and talk with my uncle I've learned something. What comes to mind is I was walking to the cafeteria as a freshman at Bowie state and my uncle was standing in front of the bookstore with a purple jacket on talking to someone. I knew very little about him being in a fraternity or his connection to education. We talked about HBCU's being a family tradition and history and what I could expect while at school. We spoke about sports, family pride and the balance necessary to be a student athlete. He shook my hand and walked off. We have continued to have brief conversations that matter throughout my life. There was another time when my wife and I bumped into him and Aunt Cardrienne in Sam's club and I had a pack of chicken thighs in my cart. Uncle James went on to explain how the skin of the chicken over time would cause impotence and right at that moment Trashawn grabbed the chicken and put it back. We all had a good laugh about that. It was a lighthearted exchange, but the message was clear that he didn't want us eating as much meat as had been. - **Marcus Quinn Noel**

Jim and I have been friends for over 50 yrs. So many memories and funny jokes I could tell, "laughing when I think of so many good times." Jim is a loyal friend.

Charles Robinson

Someone once said, show me the man you honor and I will know what kind of man you are. I can't thank you enough for how grateful I am to have had you and Cardrienne in my life. You and your family were like the real-life Huxtables from the Cosby Show to me. I have always borrowed and applied your life skills and sense of family to mold how I would raise my own. Showing me the right path, to live a simple life and always find what's important to me.

Even when I stumbled and fell, you told me to pick myself up and keep fighting. You told me once that "experience is not what happens to you; it is what you do with what happens to you". Those words stuck with me and continue to resonate. You've been a trusted advisor and kept me acutely aware of my strength as a man and my esteemed pride as a black man. You've instilled an entrepreneurial spirit in me and told me to chase my dreams and work towards my ambition. You have always been instrumental in my career and allowed me to peek over your shoulder to see how you moved in business.

As far as the community and activism, the leadership that you exemplified gave me something to aspire to. Watching you do what you love and seeing you make a difference in the lives of others is an incredible experience. I would not be the person I am today without your guidance. You continue to inspire me to become an even better version of myself. It is my sincerest wish to be to someone, what you've been to me. **Larry Young**

"What A Man," "What A Man," "What A Mighty Good Man!"

For the celebration of **Mr. James Griffin's** 80th birthday, I recall the theme song selection that would fill the atmosphere as he was escorted into the venue. Three simple phrases, **"What A Man," "What A Man," "What A Mighty Good Man"** provided a kaleidoscope of attributes, bright and promising as a rainbow, for such a Gentle Giant, **Mr. James Griffin, "What A Man"** to take the challenges and lessons of very humble beginnings and embark upon an unpredictable journey to ultimately become the owner and proprietor of an organization with healing competence, **"What A Man,"** to devote a lifetime to community activism, support of those in need and the rendering of profound knowledge to all generations, **"What A Mighty Good Man,"** to manifest unconditional love and consistent public displays of affection from his Queen, Mrs. Cardrienne Griffin, for 60 years and to provide one hundred percent, in every way for his family, while continuously empowering countless others.

This modest tribute represents a group of individuals who have been influenced by the character of **Mr. Griffin** for approximately 40 years. His kindness, humorous nature, infectious laugh, intellect, commitment to justice for all, peaceful demeanor, persistence, athletic prose, service orientation, and determination to forever make a difference for the world have positively impacted our lives in many ways.

Papa Griffin, it has been spoken that "Our lives begin to end the day we become silent about things that matter." Therefore, your years of verbal and non-verbal lessons bestowed upon the generations will live on forever. We thank you for your inspiration and for being such a great example of "**A Mighty Good Man.**»

Lovingly,

Glynis Ross, Janet Branch, Marcia Lamb Pope, Bernard Lundy Jr., Rebertha Pope-Matthews, Irene Smith, Lori Adair Chambers, Melody Harris, your sons and daughters of Forever Friends of VSU.

The Griffins

The wedding party
Cardrienne and James Griffin

Cardrienne and
James Griffin

Young Jim

Young Cardrienne

Funeral service for Debbie April 5, 2014 at Bethel AME Church. Members of Alpha Kappa Alpha Sorority lined up outside to get into the Ivy Beyond the Wall Ceremony. That line wrapped around the block with hundreds of AKA's.

Jewel, Cardrienne, Cheryl - Atlanta AKA Convention 2014

Overjoyed at welcoming Jada into our family AKA legacy and sisterhood at North Carolina A&T University in 2017.

Cheryl, Jewel, Jada, Cardrienne

Cheryl, Debbie, Cardrienne and Jewel all pledged at Virginia State University, Alpha Epsilon Chapter.

Daughters Cheryl and Jewel became inducted into WO-BE-CO, Inc. (May 2019)

WO-BE-CO, Inc. members
Jewel is President and Cheryl is Vice President.

Modern Granny Affair at The Forum in Balto. One of Cardrienne's many social clubs she belonged to.

In our home.

Griffin Family Reunion. What was being said???

Good times in our home!

Griffin Family Reunion Aug. 2015

Family Cookout in Richmond, Va.

Family celebrating Jackie's 40th Birthday in Baltimore March 2019.

Jim and Jamal share the same birthday March 11.

Seated- Jay Jr., PopPop, Coral, Jamal; Standing Sean, Jarvis, Riley, Dominique. Celebrating Jay Jrs. 30th Birthday in Alexander, Va. Aug. 2019.

| Jasmine (Malcolm & Sonya's Daughter) and Big Mama | Great grandson Jeremiah with poppop in Richmond, Va. at Cheryl's home. Jeremiah was born 9/24/19 to Jarvis and Destiny. | At Biden's home. President Biden and Jarvis (son of Cheryl & Jay Sr.). Biden was VP when this was taken at Bidens home when Jarvis and the University of Delaware won the CAA in 2014. |

Cousins celebrating Dominique's 25th Birthday.
Jay Jr. (Oldest son of Cheryl & Jay), Coral (Jewel and Eric's daughter), Dominique (daughter of Malcolm and Melinda) and Sean (Malcolm and Ricca's son). Standing in back – Jarvis (Son of Cheryl & Jay)

Jada (Daughter of Debbie and Dean) with poppop.

Jim with his Omega Psi Phi friends who came to support his recognition as co-founder of WO-BE-CO

Sister Viola, Jim and Sister Ersell at Griffin Family reunion.

WOBECO's 50th Anniversary with Cheryl, Jewel, Judy Cox and Senator Jill Carter.

James and Cardrienne with close friends: Zerita Carter (wife of Walter P. Carter), Marion Patterson (wife of Roland Patterson), LaFerne Turner, and Willa Bouldin.

Jim and his friends gather at his house in 2019.

Dean Shannon, Griff and Jay Threatt, Sr. (Son in laws)

Christmas at our home

Supporting our grandson at CAA tournament 2014 in Balto.

Jim and brother Lawrence Griffin

One of the principal achievers
Dameon all grown up in 2020.

Pi Omega Chapter
Founders Award

CORE Meritorious
Service Award

Social Action Committee of Pi
Omega Chapter for service to the
African-American community

New Africa outstanding
Community Service

FOOTBALL TEAM

Cardrienne & James
and his sisters,
Elizabeth (sitting),
Ersell and Gladys.

Newspaper articles about social justice, the school board
protest, Jim being sworn in as manager of Baltimore City
School board, and Marches against Slumlords.

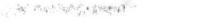

Oldest Grandson Jay Jr. Currently playing professional basketball in his 9th yr. in France.

Jeremiah, youngest grandchild(Jarvis & Destiny)

Oldest daughter also known as, "Motor Butt and Madame Butterfly"

Celebrating Cardrienne's 80th birthday
Standing left to right: Chanel, Jewel, Debbie
Seated left to right: Cheryl, Dominique, Coral and Jada

Dad and baby girl
whom he calls, "baby
cakes"

Christmas 2019

Men in Black!
Cardrienne's repass
Dean, Malcolm, Jim, Jamal,
Jay Sr. and Sean (front)

Saying so long to our Angel ♥

3 generations!

Our circle of close friends and families worshipping together and praying for strength on the anniversary of Cadrienne's funeral.

Jim Griffin

Omega Man

Made in the USA
Middletown, DE
01 July 2021